THE SOMALI ECONOMY

With a Primary Focus on the Current Thriving Sectors of the Economy

Hassan Dudde

CONTENTS

Preface 2

Abbreviations 5

Chapter One 6
A Profile of Somalia

Geography (9), People and Customs (11), Language (12), Somalia in Summary (13)

Chapter Two 15
The Somali Economy in Perspective

Introduction (18), Overview of Finance in Somalia (19), Historical Overview of the Finance / Banking Sector (21), Banking and Finance in Somalia (24), Somali Stock Exchange (33), Remittances (35), Regulation (40), Mobile Banking (41), Economic Opportunities and Investments (44), Summary (45)

Chapter Three... 44
Telecommunications and Economic Policies

Introduction (47), Overview of the Telecommunications Sector in Somalia (47), Growth of the Telecommunications Sector (49), Market Size and Key Players (51), Mobile Telecommunications and Mobile Banking (58), Internet Services in Somalia (66), Economic Benefits of Improved Telecommunications (69), Summary (71)

Chapter Four... 71
The Energy Sector

Introduction (73), Background of the Oil and Gas Sector in Somalia (74), Electricity in Somalia (75), Biomass Energy (76), Alternative Forms of

Energy in Somalia (80), Energy Sector Regulations (87), Oil and Gas Exploration in Somalia (87), Legal and Regulatory Framework (94), Economic Opportunities of Oil and Gas Exploration (95), Natural Resources and the Environment (98), Summary (99)

Chapter Five 103
Infrastructure

Introduction (104), Infrastructure in Somalia (105), Roads (108), Airports (113), Ports (119), Infrastructure Challenges Within Somalia (123), Economic Opportunities in Infrastructure (125), Key Players and Public Private Partnerships (128), Summary (131)

References 136

About the Author 145

Dedication 146

Modern Day Somalia, 2011

PREFACE

In times gone by, military strength ruled, as did the manufacture of weaponry. However, in this changing world, military no longer has a stronghold; it is now the turn of technology and economy. This is indeed an interesting era; and small nations are at the forefront. Business is no longer threatened by multinationals with hundreds of thousands of workers; a clever, diminutive operation can now take over a larger one.

This world of ours is now dominated by economics - this is a world in which Somalia can not only compete, but be a leading nation, too.

The purpose of writing this book is to educate those that know Somalia only through the sometimes-biased, one-sided viewpoint of the Media. With this book, we reach out to a new audience that wishes to do business in Somalia and sees this blossoming country as a rich and dynamic resource.
I believe that Somalia, like most of the African countries, is blessed with great natural resources and creative human capital that can be guided to advance the country.

During the period that I was writing this book, I spent a great deal of time in Somalia and had many fascinating experiences there.
 I grew up in the West and my entrepreneurial skills were fostered and honed there. Being of a go-ahead mindset, I came away from Somalia, with the desire to let everyone know about the great possibilities that this country holds.

I have been blessed to work with great people that believe in making change in this part of the world. Mr. Bashir Ali in particular, is such a person, as without his support it would not be possible to achieve this in such a short space of time. I am proud to say that I belong to the Somali Economic Forum, the organisation that made the Somali Stock Exchange (SSE) business idea a reality. As well as hosting Annual Events, the Forum also publishes insightful reports that cover all thriving sectors of Somalia; in this book, you will find details about those sectors.

The book's chapters explain each subject matter in-depth, and each chapter starts with an Introductory section, which aims to give the reader a good understanding of Somalia - from its long history to its diverse culture. We start by Introducing Somalia: a country rich in geography, customs and language. The second chapter: ***The Somali Economy in Perspective*** draws a fine picture of the country's economy, the perception and realities - as well as its current economic conditions. This is followed by **Telecommunications and Economic Policies**, which lists the policies introduced in the country after the Civil War and during the country's first permanent government in twenty years. Mobile Telecommunications are covered in great detail, as is the Internet and Mobile Banking.

In Chapter Four, **The Energy Sector** is discussed. There is a booming new industry in clean, green energy such as windmills and hydroelectricity. Old forms of energy are looked at too and the need for breakthroughs in this much-mooted sector. We also look at the regulations that abound and the recommendations made by the Somalia Economic Forum.

The final Chapter deals with Infrastructure and its impact on business and everyday life. It looks at the plans to better roads and make ports larger. This chapter also delves into the subject of Public Private Partnerships (PPP) and their role in the now stable Somalia.

Economy of Somalia revisits the history and evolution of the country's finance sector, starting from the colonial times, then moves to the 1960's, when the Central Bank of Somalia was created - although the country was mostly dependent of its foreign aid assistance and managed to hold the Somali Chilling relatively strong.

The book also highlights the financial revolution - perhaps the most visible in the modern economy: this derives from the unique change that the country has gone through, whereby many Money Transfer Organisations (MTO) started to change their business status to Commercial and Corporate Banks. These unique changes also attracted a number of foreign financial institutions, which saw Somalia as a new emerging frontier.

My wish that is that you gain great benefit from reading this book, and embrace the truth that Somali has so much to offer businesses - both homegrown and global.

Copyright © Hassan Dudde - 2019

The moral right of Hassan Dudde to be identified as the author of this work has been asserted in accordance with the Copyright, Design and Patents Act 1988.

All rights reserved, including the right to reproduce this book, or portions thereof, in any form. No part of this text may be reproduced, transmitted, downloaded, decompiled, reverse engineered, or stored in or introduced into any information storage and retrieval system, in any form and by any means, whether electronic or mechanical without the express written permission of the publisher and author. The scanning, uploading, and distribution of this book via the Internet or via any other means without the permission of the publisher is illegal and punishable by law. Please purchase only authorised electronic editions, and do not participate in or encourage electronic piracy of copyrighted materials.

HASSAN DUDDE, IN ASSOCIATION WITH
SSE PUBLISHING LTD.

Published by: SSE Publishing Ltd.
P.O. Box 20016
Garowe, PL, Somalia.

www.ssepublishing.com
info@ssepublishing.com

ABBREVIATIONS

ABEDA - Arab Bank of Economic Development in Africa
AU - African Union
CRD - Centre for Research and Dialogue
FDI - Foreign Direct Investment
FGS - Federal Government of Somalia
GDP - Gross Domestic Product
IOC - International Oil Companies
IPP - Independent Power Producers
MFI - Micro-finance Institution
MMT - Mobile Money Transfer
MTO - Money Transfer Organisations
NDP - National Development Plan
NREAP - National Renewable Energy Action Plans
PFMP - Public Finance Management Policy
PHA - Puntland Highway Authority
PPP - Public Private Partnerships
PSA - Product Sharing Agreement
PSU - Puntland State University
SCAMA - Somali Civil Aviation and Meteorological Agency
SEF - Somali Economic Forum
SFSA - Somali Financial Services Association
SOMTA - Somali Money Transfer Association
SOS - Somali Shilling
SPC - Somalia Petroleum Company
STA - Somali Telecom Association
SSE – Somali Stock Exchange
TIA - Turkish Investment Authority
UAE - United Arab Emirates
UNDP - United Nations Development Programme

CHAPTER ONE
A PROFILE OF SOMALIA

Modern History:

In 1960, northern British Somaliland voted to join southern Italian Somaliland to create Somalia. The Somalis are one of the most similar peoples in Africa. Somalia is home to 16.3m people, made up of: 85% Somali - and Bantu /other non-Somali (15%).

The CIA reports that there are 5.663 billion cu m of proven natural gas reserves, and, according to the Central Bank of Somalia, the growing economy is expected to not only match its pre-Civil War levels, but also to accelerate in growth and development. This is due to Somalia's untapped natural resources, which include: uranium, iron ore, tin, gypsum, bauxite, copper, salt and natural gas.

Somalia has a strong infrastructure; with sixty-two airports in various cities across Somalia which accommodate aerial transportation. Somalia also has the longest coastline on the continent, and several major seaports. The port cities are: Mogadishu, Bosaso, Berbera, Kismayo and Merca.

Geography:

Somalia is a semi-arid land in the Horn of Africa. It is flat to the south, with mountains in the north reaching more than 2,000 meters (6,500 feet).

Somalia is bordered by Djibouti to the northwest, Kenya to the southwest, the Gulf of Aden to the north, the Indian Ocean to the east, and Ethiopia to the west.
The country lies between latitudes 2°S and 12°N, and longitudes 41° and 52°E.

Somalia is strategically located at the mouth of the Bab el Mandeb gateway to the Red Sea and the Suez Canal. The nation has a total area of 637,657 square kilometres (246,201 sq mi) of which constitutes land, with 10,320 square kilometres (3,980 sq mi) of water. Somalia's land boundaries extend to about 2,340 kilometres (1,450 mi); 58 kilometres (36 mi) of that is shared with Djibouti, 682 kilometres (424 mi) with Kenya, and 1,626 kilometres (1,010 mi) with Ethiopia. Its maritime claims include territorial waters of 200 nautical miles (370 km; 230 mi).

Somalia has several islands and archipelagos on its coast, including the Bajuni Islands and the Saad ad-Din Archipelago.

In the north, a scrub-covered, semi-desert plain referred as the *Guban* lies parallel to the Gulf of Aden littoral. With a width of twelve kilometres in the west to as little as two kilometres in the east, the plain is bisected by watercourses that are essentially beds of dry sand - except during the rainy seasons. When the rains arrive, the Guban's low bushes and grass clumps transform into lush vegetation.

Cal Madow is a mountain range in the north-eastern part of the country. Extending from several kilometres west of the city of Bosaso to the northwest of Erigavo, it features Somalia's highest peak, Shimbiris, which sits at an elevation of about 2,416 metres (7,927 ft).

The rugged east-west ranges of the Karkaar Mountains also lie to the interior of the Gulf of Aden littoral. In the central regions, the country's northern mountain ranges give way to shallow plateaus and typically dry watercourses that are referred to locally as the *Ogo*. The Ogo's western plateau, in turn, gradually merges into the Haud, an important grazing area for livestock.

Somalia has only two permanent rivers, the Jubba and Shabele, both of which begin in the Ethiopian Highlands. These rivers mainly flow southwards, with the Jubba River entering the Indian Ocean at Kismayo. The Shabele River, at one time, used to enter the sea near Merca, but now reaches a point just southwest of Mogadishu.

There are four main seasons around which pastoral and agricultural life revolve, and these are dictated by shifts in the wind patterns. From December to March is the *Jilal*, the harshest dry season of the year. The main rainy season, referred to as the *Gu*, lasts from April to June. This period is characterised by the southwest monsoons, which rejuvenate the pastureland, especially the central plateau. From July to September is the second dry season, the *Xagaa* (pronounced "Hagaa"). The *Dayr*, which is the shortest rainy season, lasts from October to December.

The *tangambili* periods that intervene between the two monsoons (October–November and March–May) are hot and humid.

Somalia contains a variety of mammals due to its geographical and climatic diversity. Wild fauna includes: cheetah, lion, reticulated giraffe, baboon, civet, elephant, bushpig, ibex, kudu, dik-dik, reedbuck and zebra, shrew, rock hyrax, golden mole and antelope. It also has a large population of the dromedary camel.

Somalia is currently home to around 727 species of birds. Somalia's territorial waters are prime fishing grounds for highly migratory marine species, such as tuna.

People and Customs:

About 85% of local residents are ethnic Somalis, who have historically inhabited the northern part of the country. They have traditionally been organised into nomadic pastoral clans, loose empires, sultanates and city-states.

Non-Somali ethnic minority groups make up the remainder of Somalia's population, and are largely concentrated in the southern regions:
Bravanese, Bantus, Bajuni, Ethiopians, Indians, Persians, Italians, and Britons.

Somalia's population is expanding at a growth rate of 1.75% per annum and a birth rate of 40.87 births/1,000 people. Most local residents are young, with a median age of 17.7 years; about 44% of the population is between the ages of 0–14 years, 52.4% is between the ages of 15–64 years, and only 2.3% is 65 years of age or older. The gender ratio is evenly balanced.

The rate of urbanization is approximately 4.79% per annum (2005–10 est.), with many towns quickly growing into cities. Many ethnic minorities have also moved from rural areas to urban centres, particularly to Mogadishu, Kismayo and other fast growing cities of Garowe and Boss. As of 2008, 37.7% of the nation's population live in towns and cities, with the percentage rapidly increasing.

The cuisine of Somalia varies from region to region and is a mixture of diverse culinary influences. This is due to Somalia's rich tradition of trade and commerce. Despite the variety, there remains one thing that unites the various regional cuisines: all food is served halal. There are therefore no pork dishes, alcohol is not served, nothing that died on its own is eaten, and no blood is incorporated.

Varieties of *bariis* (rice), the most popular probably being basmati, usually act as the main dish. Cumin, cardamom, cloves, cinnamon and garden sage are used to aromatize these different rice dishes.

Somalis serve dinner as late as 9 pm and during Ramadan, supper is often presented after Tarawih prayers; sometimes up to 11 pm. After meals, homes are traditionally perfumed using frankincense (*lubaan*) or incense (*cuunsi*), which is prepared inside an incense burner referred to as a *dabqaad*.

Language:

Somali and Arabic are the official languages of Somalia. The Somali language is the mother tongue of the Somali people, the nation's largest ethnic group. Somali is the best documented of the Cushitic languages, with academic studies dating it from before 1900. The English language is becoming the most commonly used business language in Somalia; over 60% of the young work force communicates in English.

Somali dialects are divided into three main groups: Northern, Benadir and Maay. Northern Somali (or Northern-Central Somali) forms the basis for Standard Somali. Benadir (also known as Coastal Somali) is spoken on the Benadir coast, from Adale to south of Merca, including Mogadishu, as well as in the immediate hinterland. Maay is principally spoken by the Digil and Mirifle (Rahanweyn) clans in the southern areas of Somalia.

In addition to Somali, Arabic, is an official national language. Many Somalis speak it due to centuries-old ties with the Arab world, the far-reaching influence of the Arabic Media, and religious education.

English is widely spoken and taught; it used to be a working language in the British Somaliland protectorate. Italian was an official language in Italian Somaliland, during the trusteeship period, but its use significantly diminished following independence. It is now most frequently heard among older generations.

Somalia in Summary:

Somalia comprises of 27 regions and was colonized by both Britain and France before it gained independence in July 1, 1960. It was formed from the merger of the British colony of the Somali Italia and British Somalia.. In 1991, Somalia's Central Government collapsed and civil war began, which lasted for over two decades.

Somalia has a very rich history and it has been inhabited since at least the Paleolithic Age. The currency of Somalia is the Somali Shilling or SOS, which has been in use since 1962. The Federal Parliament of Somalia is the national parliament of Somalia, the bicameral National Legislature, consisting of House of Representatives (lower house) and senate (upper house). whose members are elected to serve four-year terms. The parliament elects the President, Speaker of Parliament and Deputy Speakers. It also has the authority to pass and veto laws. Somalia's foreign relations are handled by the President as the head of state, the Prime Minister as the head of government, and the federal Ministry of Foreign Affairs. Mogadishu is arguably the largest city in the country and it's where the Federal Government resides. *It is also known as Xamar.*

After the start of the civil war, various new telecommunications companies began to spring up and compete to provide missing infrastructure. Funded by Somali entrepreneurs and backed by expertise from China, Korea and Europe, these telecommunications firms offer affordable mobile phone and Internet services that are not available in many other parts of the continent. Customers can conduct money transfers (such as through the popular Dahabshiil) and other banking activities via mobile phones, as well as easily gain wireless Internet access.

After forming partnerships with multinational corporations such as Sprint, ITT and Telenor, these firms now offer the cheapest and clearest phone calls in Africa. These Somali telecommunication companies also provide services to every city, town and hamlet in Somalia.

There are presently around 25 mainlines per 1,000 persons, and the local availability of telephone lines (*tele-density*) is higher than in neighbouring countries; three times greater than in adjacent Ethiopia.

Prominent Somali telecommunications companies include: Golis Telecom Group, Hormuud Telecom, Somafone, Nationlink, Netco, Telcom and Somali Telecom Group.

Hormuud Telecom alone grosses about $40 million a year. Despite their rivalry, several of these companies signed an interconnectivity deal in 2005 that allows them to set prices, maintain and expand their networks, and ensure that competition does not get out of control.

Investment in the telecom industry is held to be one of the clearest signs that Somalia's economy has continued to develop. The sector provides key communication services, and in the process facilitates job creation and income generation.

The state-run Somali National Television is the principal national public service TV channel. After a 20-year hiatus, the station was officially relaunched on 4 April 2011. Its radio counterpart, Radio Mogadishu, also broadcasts from the capital. Somaliland National TV and Puntland TV and Radio air from the northern regions.

Additionally, Somalia has several private television and radio networks. Among these are Horn Cable Television and Universal TV. The political Xog Doon and Xog Ogaal and Horyaal Sports broadsheets publish out of the capital. There are also a number of online media outlets covering local news, including Garowe Online, Wardheernews, and Puntland Post.

The Internet country code top-level domain (ccTLD) for Somalia is **.so**.
It was officially relaunched on 1 November 2010 by **.SO Registry**, which is regulated by the nation's Ministry of Posts and Telecommunications.

On 22 March 2012, the Somali Cabinet also unanimously approved the **National Communications Act**. The bill paves the way for the establishment of a National Communications regulator in the broadcasting and telecommunications sectors.

The Central Bank of Somalia is the official monetary authority of Somalia and, in terms of financial management, it is in the process of assuming the task of both formulating and implementing monetary policy.

The US dollar is widely accepted as a medium of exchange alongside the Somali shilling. Although Somalia has had no central monetary authority for more than 15 years between the outbreak of the civil war in 1991 and the subsequent re-establishment of the Central Bank of Somalia in 2009, the nation's payment system is fairly advanced primarily due to the widespread existence of private money transfer operators (MTO) that have acted as informal banking networks.

These remittance firms (*hawalas*) have become a large industry in Somalia, with an estimated $1.6 billion USD annually remitted to the region by Somalis in the diaspora via money transfer companies. Most are members of the Somali Money Transfer Association (SOMTA), an umbrella organisation that regulates the community's money transfer sector, or its predecessor, the Somali Financial Services Association (SFSA). The largest of the Somali MTOs is Dahabshiil, a Somali-owned firm employing more than 2000 people across 144 countries with branches in London and Dubai.

With a significant improvement in local security, Somali expatriates began returning to the country for investment opportunities. Coupled with modest foreign investment, the inflow of funds have helped the Somali shilling increase considerably in value. By March 2014, the currency had appreciated by almost 60% against the U.S. dollar over the previous 12 months. The Somali shilling was the strongest among the 175 global currencies traded by Bloomberg, rising close to 50 percentage points higher than the next most robust global currency over the same period.

According to the CIA and the Central Bank of Somalia, despite experiencing civil unrest, Somalia has maintained a healthy informal economy, based mainly on livestock, remittance/money transfer companies and telecommunications.

In 2009, the CIA estimated that the GDP had grown to $5.731 billion, with a projected real growth rate of 2.6%. According to a 2007 British Chambers of Commerce report, the private sector also grew, particularly in the service sector.

There has been substantial private investment in commercial activities; this has been largely financed by the Somali diaspora, and includes trade and marketing, money transfer services, transportation, communications, fishery equipment, airlines, telecommunications, education, health, construction and hotels.

Libertarian economist Peter Leeson attributes this increased economic activity to the Somali customary law (referred to as Xeer), which he suggests provides a stable environment to conduct business in.

Somalia's economy consists of both traditional and modern production, with a gradual shift toward modern industrial techniques. Agriculture is the most important economic sector of Somalia. It accounts for about 65% of the GDP and employs 65% of the workforce. Livestock contributes about 40% to GDP and more than 50% of export earnings.

With the advantage of being located near the Arabian Peninsula, Somali traders have increasingly begun to challenge Australia's traditional dominance over the Gulf Arab livestock and meat market, offering quality animals at very low prices. In response, Gulf Arab states have started to make strategic investments in the country, with Saudi Arabia building livestock export infrastructure and the United Arab Emirates purchasing large farmlands. Somalia is also a major world supplier of frankincense and myrrh.

According to the Somali Chamber of Commerce and Industry, over six private airline firms also offer commercial flights to both domestic and international locations, including Daallo Airlines, Jubba Airways, African Express Airways, East Africa 540, Central Air and Hajara.

In 2008, the Puntland government signed a multimillion-dollar deal with Dubai's Lootah Group, a regional industrial group operating in the Middle East and Africa. According to the agreement, the first phase of the investment is worth Dhs 170 m and will see a set of new companies established to operate, manage and build Bosaso's free trade zone and sea and airport facilities.

The Bosaso Airport Company is slated to develop the airport complex to meet international standards, including a new 3,400 m

(11,200 ft) runway, main and auxiliary buildings, taxi and apron areas, and security perimeters.
In 2004, an $8.3 million *Coca-Cola* bottling plant opened in Mogadishu, with investors hailing from various constituencies in Somalia.

Foreign investment also included multinationals including General Motors and Dole Fruit.

Business is booming in Somalia!

CHAPTER TWO

THE SOMALI ECONOMY IN PERSPECTIVE

Introduction:

One of the main objectives of the organisation I have served: the **Somali Economic Forum** - has always been to promote sustainable economic development in Somalia and central to this is the development of Somalia's financial sector.

Somalis are an entrepreneurial people by their nature and, as a result; a responsive and strong financial and banking sector will enable the economy to benefit from such entrepreneurial activity. Indeed, a robust financial and banking sector is a necessity for an economy to function and prosper and is one of a set of interconnected structural elements that provide a framework for conducive economic development. This chapter's facts have been collated by conducting in-depth economic research on the financial houses, formal banks, commercial banks and remittance firms already existing within Somalia - and the financial needs of Somalia as a state.

In the past couple of years, Somalia has experienced an economic and political renaissance, which has encouraged sustained investment in various sectors. Perhaps the sector with the most potential is the finance sector.

I believe wholeheartedly that a focused strategy on developing financial and formal banking institutions of the state will play a crucial role in fostering economic growth and creating jobs. I also believe that increased efficiency and investment in Somalia's financial sector will help to transform Somalia rapidly in terms of its economy. It is for this reason that we have provided recommendations in terms of Somalia's financial development.

Crucially, with the prominence of remittance firms in Somalia's macroeconomic, as well as microeconomic growth, we have dedicated a section on remittances as a form of finance within Somalia.

I would like to reserve special thanks to my **Somali Economic Forum** colleagues - based in our offices across Somalia - as their focus and valued collaboration assisted us in our completion of this chapter.

1. Overview of Finance in Somalia

Somalia's 22 years of internal strife has culminated in the country resiliently functioning amidst: collapsed central state institutions, faltering social and economic infrastructure and considerable levels of internal and external migration[1]. Nonetheless, against all odds, he traditional Somali spirit of entrepreneurship and commerce has remained resolute throughout and the private sector in Somalia is, according to economic experts; robust and expanding rapidly. Indeed, the private sector has managed to grow impressively in the past two decades, predominantly in the areas of: trade, remittance services and telecommunications. It is also important to note that the primary sectors and backbone of Somalia's economy, notably livestock, agriculture and fisheries, are also gaining new economic momentum too. Agriculture is the single most significant sector in terms of the employment and the overall economy, with livestock accounting for about 40% of GDP and more than 50% of export earnings. Nomads and semi-pastoralists, which are dependent upon livestock for their living, make up a large percentage of the population. Livestock, hides, fish, charcoal, rice, sugarcane and bananas are Somalia's principal exports, while sugar, sorghum, corn, khat, and machined goods are the primary imports.

Somalia also possesses a nascent industrial sector, based on the processing of agricultural products. Somalia, in its heyday, had a powerful industrial base which was utilised extensively by the then Socialist government. Yet, due to the civil war and instability of the past two decades, industrial machinery and goods have largely been looted and the machinery sold as scrap metal, hampering the industrial development of the nation. In contrast, Somalia's service sector has witnessed steady growth and development with a wide range of private sector businesses flourishing in the unregulated, less bureaucratic, free-market environment. Unlike the pre-civil war period, when most services and the industrial

---

[1] United Nations Development Programme/World Bank Somalia, Socio-Economic Statistics, Somalia, Report No 1 Somalia Watching Brief 2003, draft

sector were government-run, there has been considerable private investment in commercial activities; largely financed by the Somali diaspora and this includes: trade, money transfer services, transportation, communications, fishery equipment, airlines, telecommunications, education, health, as well as construction and hotels. Telecommunication firms provide wireless services in most major cities and offer the lowest international call rates on the continent; possibly worldwide, too.

Yet, Somalia's financial sector is underdeveloped and characterised by the absence of a formal banking sector, instead remittance firms handling various money transfer services have appeared throughout the country, handling up to £1.4 billion in remittances annually. In Somalia, one could argue that remittance firms have positioned themselves strategically to benefit from the lack of a formal banking sector. However, it is important to note that, with the stabilisation of Somalia in recent years and due to increased economic activities, spearheaded by the diaspora, there is now a flourishing and simple banking sector emerging. Indeed, this theme of the diaspora providing finance for various economic activities can be extended to the rebirth of Somalia's capital city, Mogadishu, which has enabled the city to undergo considerable development and the explosion of the services sector. This in turn has led to the opening of various diaspora-led investments and ventures such as: new hotels, gas stations, supermarkets, and flight networks to Europe (i.e. Istanbul-Mogadishu) with many new flight networks planned in the near future.

Additionally, Mogadishu's main market "Bakara Market" continues to offer a variety of goods from food to the latest electronic gadgets. This economic growth has occurred not just in Mogadishu but across the entire nation, especially in densely populated cities like Kismayo, Bosaso and Hargeisa - which have also benefited from increased economic activity initiated by diaspora financing.

1.1 Historical Overview of the Finance / Banking Sector

The following summary details the various institutions that have provided formal banking services in Somalia since 1920:[2]

1920 Banca d'Italia (Central Bank of Italy) establishes its branch in Mogadishu. It is the first bank to open in Southern Somalia.

1925 Banca d'Italia opens another branch in Kismayo on the 2nd November 1925.

1930 The British Government opens the Government Savings Bank in Northern Somalia with the objectives to encourage the locals to save parts of their income

1932 In Mogadishu a branch of Cassa di Risparmio di Torino, an Italian commercial Bank, opens its office.

1936 A branch of Banco di Roma, an Italian commercial bank, is established in Mogadishu. In the same year Banca d'Italia opens its third branch in the city of Merca.

1938 Banco di Napoli takes over the branch of Cassa di Risparmio di Torino branch in Mogadishu.

1941 All Italian banks are closed by the British Administration.

1943 The Barclays Bank DCO, a British Commercial Bank, is opened in Mogadishu, this coincides with a time when the British Government Army is taking control of the southern regions of Somalia.

1950 Italian commercial banks, such as Banco di Roma and Banco di Napoli reopen their branches in Mogadishu.

1950 The Italian Trusteeship Administration (A.F.I.S.) establishes on 8th April, 1950 a new currency institution regulator

---

[2] https://www.cia.gov/library/publications/the-world-factbook/geos/so.html#Econ. 2008. CIA World Fact Book

" Cassa perla circolazionemonetaria della Somalia" with its head quarter in Rome. Main functions of the new institution are:

a) **Treasury services**
b) **Advances to A.F.I.S. for short-term loan**
c) **Issuance of circular cheques and current accounts' cheques**
d) **Acceptance of deposits from the public**
e) **Buying and selling foreign currencies and gold**
f) **Buying and selling government bonds**
g) **Rediscounting commercial bank's bills**
h) **Invest its assets, except cash kept as guarantee**

1952 A branch of National Bank of India, a commercial bank owned by the British Government opens in Hargeysa.

1954 The National Bank of India opens another branch in Berbera.

1960 the Central Bank of Somalia establishes the **"Somali National Bank"** by Decree No.3 of 30 June, 1960 and converted into Law No.2 of 13 January, 1961.

The Somali National Bank is authorised to extend its activities to all regions of the Republic of Somalia and goes ahead to the following branches:
- **Hargeisa – 20 August 1961**
- **Berbera – 27 January 1962**
- **Kismayo – 5 November 1962**
- **Bosaso – 26 March 1963**
- **Qardho – 26 March 1963**
- **Burao – 29 March 1963**
- **Galkaio – 5 November 1963**
- **Baidoa – 4 January 1965**
- **Beled Weyne – 6 January 1965**

The Somali National Bank being a Central Bank was not allowed to carry commercial banking operations, but due to the non-presence of commercial banks in most of the regions of the country, the Government of Somalia enacted Decree No.264 of 3rd November, 1962 bestowing on the Somali National Bank the authority to engage in commercial banking operations.

1961 Banque de Port Said, an Egyptian commercial bank, opens a branch in Mogadishu, and operates until 7th of May, 1970.

1968 The Somali Development Bank is established by Decree No.2 of 28th February 1968.
Art. 3 of the Law states that the Bank's main purpose for its establishment is to play a significant financial role to all economic sectors in medium and long-term loans, in particular agriculture, industry, mining and tourism. The Somali Development Bank as per Art. No. 5 of its foundation act was not allowed to accept deposits or savings from the depositors.

1968 The National and Grindlays Bank establishes a new branch. The Bank also starts operations in Hargeisa and Berbera.

1968 the Credito Somalo is closed due to a liquidity crisis and all its assets and liabilities are transferred to the Somali National Bank. On the 7th of May, 1970 all foreign commercial banks are nationalized[3].

1971 The establishment of two public commercial banks. On the 1st January, 1971 two commercial banks are established:
1. **Somali Savings and Credit Bank**
2. **Somali Commercial Bank**

The two banks are autonomous institutions with legal personalities and a capital of So.Shs. 2,500,000 each of which 50% is paid by the Somali Government and 50% by the Central Bank of Somalia.

The two institutions are fully owned by the Government, with same objectives and activities (commercial banks), their operation are based on deposits and savings and short-term loans.

1975 In 1975 a change to the structure of banking system in Somalia is introduced. The two commercial banks are amalgamated into the Commercial and Savings Bank of Somalia, at the same time, the Somali National Bank is renamed the Central Bank of Somalia.

1990 In 1990 following an agreement with the I.M.F. on 1st July, 1990 the Government implements IMF private sector reforms.

---

[3] http://www.nationsencyclopedia.com/Africa/Somalia-BANKING-AND-SECURITIES.html. Somalia - Banking and Securities.

These reforms lead to market oriented policies and the establishment of a new commercial bank; Somali Commercial Bank by Presidential Decree No. 4 of 16 December, 1989, with a capital of So.Shs. 2 billion divided into two thousand shares of one million So.Shs each. One billion is paid jointly by the Government and the Central Bank of Somalia and one billion are left to the private investors of which only 22 shares are subscribed.

2. Banking and Finance in Somalia

The collapse of the central government in Somalia in 1991 gave way to the ultimate collapse of its formal and commercial banking sector. There are currently no formal financial institutions operating in Somalia nor any fully functioning formal financial sector regulatory bodies. The absence of a formal banking sector has significantly constrained Somalia's private sector in terms of its ability to access credit and other financial services. Furthermore, the scarcity of capital has made it impossible to encourage and harness domestic savings amongst the populace. According to the UNDP and World Bank this has also had negative macroeconomic repercussions: *"...the long absence of a national government has further prevented access to international capital markets as well as the establishment of economic management institutions and regulatory bodies"* (UNDP/World Bank Somalia, 2003.)

A reform of the national currency is currently a high priority for the Somali authorities who possess a mandate with the advent of Somalia's first properly functioning government in two decades, this can actually be realized as authorities press the Central Bank of Somalia for an early issuance of a new national currency to replace the bank notes of the Somali shilling that have been in circulation for more than 20 years. The Central Bank of Somalia has not issued new bank notes since 1990 and all the new bank notes that have been in circulation are non-official, most of them being issued by self-governing regions across Somalia. Indeed, the Somali Economic Forum believes that the Federal Government of Somalia should be advised to consider introducing the new currency at a later stage, as it would require time - because of technical considerations (design, printing, and most importantly; the required legislation, etc.) and even more important, because of the need to establish sound and credible financial policies and an adequate institutional and legal framework to support the value of the new currency.

Within Somalia, the burgeoning formal banking sector is undergoing an upturn in fortunes, especially with the recent trend of remittance companies restructuring as banks. Currently, the largest player in the domestic Somali commercial banking industry is Salaam Bank, which has a considerable presence throughout various parts of Somalia. It is followed by other banks such as: Amal Bank and Dahabshill Bank, which have both experienced expansion in recent years. In particular Dahabshiil Bank has proved to be the most far-reaching and innovative, with important bases in key urban cities such as: Mogadishu, Hargeisa and Djibouti.

It is important to remember that the banking sector in Somalia is still in its early stages and, as a result, statistics regarding its activities are scarce. Despite this, economists would argue that the opportunity cost for entrants into the banking sector will indeed prove to be significant and potentially lucrative, due to projected rises in the middle classes in Somalia and increased numbers of diaspora returnees.

As mentioned earlier, the banking sector in Somalia is still very much underdeveloped, however, there is a growing percentage of Somalis who have access to and use domestic banking services in their day-to-day activities. Statistics vary but roughly 30% of Somalis use banking - it's often exclusive to the ever-growing middle-class within Somalia. This middle-class includes: a vibrant business community within the major urban centres and middle-class professionals such as teachers and government officials - who have banking accounts in order to be paid. This middle-class group also includes diaspora returnees from North America, Europe or the Middle East who are involved in various economic activities acting as a multiplier effect.

When examining the potential of the banking sector in Somalia, it is crucial to understand the growing middle classes within Somalia and per capita income in Somalia as this has led to an increased demand from these groups for loans to finance their economic activities.

Per capita income varies across Somalia, but overall it is considered to be around USD$600[4] however, within other regions of Somalia such as Puntland, statistics suggest that it has a per capita income rate of £1200[5]. Nevertheless, the overall Somalia per capita income of USD$600 is still considerably higher than other East African states such as; Ethiopia and Eritrea which is US$370 and US$403 respectively according to the World Bank. [6] Furthermore, the banking sector in Somalia tends to be unregulated and therefore when setting up shop; new banks often face little entry barriers. However, the regulation environment may change with the decision of the Federal Government of Somalia to pass and implement banking reforms through the Central Bank of Somalia. In particular, successive Central Bank Governors have called for an increased regulatory framework for domestic banks[7]. Therefore, it will be interesting to see how these domestic banks restructure in order to meet these impeding regulations.

Domestic Somali banks currently do not face consistent or significant taxation from the government, due to the institutional weakness of the government, however, with the increased powers of the Central Bank, they most likely will in the near future.

Somalia is a nation without a formal commercial banking sector which can be traced back to the overthrow of Siad Barre's government in 199. Since this period; Somalia has become too dependent and overly reliant on the remittances sector. Immediately prior to the civil war, Somalia's formal financial sector was composed of[8]:

1. **Central Bank of Somalia**
2. **Commercial and Savings Bank (in itself created**
    a. **through government's forced consolidation of a**
    b. **number of banks)**
3. **Somali Development Bank**
4. **State Insurance Company.**

---

[4] https://www.cia.gov/library/publications/the-world-factbook/geos/so.html

[5] According to statistics from Puntland State University (PSU, 2012) and UNDP

[6] http://www.worldbank.org/en/country/ethiopia/overview
http://www.worldbank.org/en/country/eritrea/overview

[7] http://www.keydmedia.net/en/news/article/somali_president_appoints_first_female_central_bank_governor/

[8] Somali Democratic Republic, Directorate of Planning, Ministry of National Planning, The Five Year National Development Plan, 1986-1991, September 1987.

Local & Regional (Informal) Banks Operating in Somalia

Dahabshiil Bank	First Somali Bank	Salaam Somali Bank
Amal Bank	Dayax Islamic Bank	Salaam Puntland Bank
Iman Bank	Iftin Bank	Barwaqo Bank

Very little information is available about the performance of banks prior to 1990. By 1991 these institutions had collapsed either as a result of bankruptcy or as a result of the collapse of state institutions and basic infrastructure. Historically, the Somali banking system is reported to have been plagued by excessive state controls and involvement, as well as gross mismanagement. In the absence of a formal financial sector in Somalia, the informal financial sector has, to some extent, filled this void. The latter has traditionally been comprised of remittance companies.

The remittance sector in Somalia dates back several decades. The scale and scope of remittances has been closely linked to Somalia's role as a source of labour for the Arabian Gulf and to the Somali Diaspora that has flourished in the West[9].

Civil unrest, insecurity and absence of a formal banking sector has proven to be a major hindrance and obstacle to the economic development of the nation. Even though the remittance sector plays a vital role in the current Somali economy, the existing financial sector can be characterised in the following:

- **Virtual lack of financial intermediation i.e. deposit-taking and lending through financial intermediaries, although some limited lending does take place through non-governmental organisations in the form of micro-finance.**

- **The economy is predominantly cash-based and heavily dollarized.**

---
[9] Remittance companies and money transfers in Somalia, Ken Menkhaus, October, 2001.

- **Lack of public confidence in a banking system especially where the government is involved. This is not surprising given that the public have had their funds squandered in the past. Hence, the revival of the banking system will depend on regaining public confidence to a very large extent.**

- **The provision of very limited banking services, such as money transfers, foreign exchange and deposit facilities, provided by the remittance companies operating informally.**

The banking sector in Somalia currently comprises of an active informal sector and a virtually non-existent formal sector. The formal banking sector in Somalia is now largely defunct due to 20 years of statelessness, their operations (or former set-ups) are listed as follows:

Commercial and Savings Bank of Somalia: In 1971, two commercial banks were established: the Somali Savings and Credit Bank and the Somali Commercial Bank. The two banks were autonomous institutions with legal personalities and a capital of 2,500,000 Somali Shillings each of which 50% paid by the Somali Government and 50% by the Central Bank of Somalia. The two institutions were fully owned by the Government, with same objectives and activities (commercial banks), their operations were based on deposits and savings and short-term loans. In 1975, following a change to the structure of the banking system in Somalia, the Government merged Somali Commercial Bank and Somali Savings and Credit Bank to form Commercial and Savings Bank of Somalia, the only bank in the Country at that time. In 1990, the nationalized Commercial and Savings Bank of Somalia failed.[10]

Somali Development Bank: The Somali Development Bank was established in 1968. Its main purpose was to play a significant financial role to all economic sectors in medium and long-term loans, in particular to the agriculture, industry, mining, and tourism sectors. As part of its foundation act, the bank was not

---

[10] http://somalbanca.org/financial-institutions/brief-history-of-the-somali-financial-institutions.html. Brief History of the Somali Financial Institutions. Central Bank of Somalia.

allowed to accept deposits or savings from depositors.[11] It has been defunct since 1991, when it collapsed along with the rest of the banking system at that time.

Somali Commercial Bank: In 1990, following an agreement with the IMF implementing a free private oriented economy, a new Somali Commercial Bank was established, with a capital of 2 billion Somali Shillings. This capital was divided into 2,000 shares of one million Somali Shillings each. One billion was paid jointly by the Government and the Central Bank of Somali and one billion was left to private investors, of which only 22 shares were subscribed.[12] The bank failed in 1991 as a result of the civil war, together with the formal financial system of the Country.

Central Bank of Somalia: The Central Bank of Somalia is unable to regulate the banking system and enjoys little autonomy. Nevertheless, there have been recent efforts to re-assert its authority over the economy and re-engage the levers over monetary policy. Despite the ongoing crises confronting Somalia, its government was commended by the UN for having put in place more transparent and accountable financial management measures. In a move that should help generate greater donor confidence, Somalia contracted auditing firm PricewaterhouseCoopers to assist with tracking and reporting on the use of public funds and thus help improve transparency, the UN reported in July 2009.

According to the Central Bank's website: *"On the monetary policy management, the newly revived Central Bank of Somalia is in the process of taking full charge of formulating and implementing monetary policy."*

Speedy resumption of taking charge of monetary policy by the Central Bank is however handicapped by lack of adequate resources, both financial and material.

Alongside the Somali shilling, the US dollar is also widely accepted as a medium of large and high transactions even for local trade exchanges i.e., the economy is deeply dollarized in view of weak

---

[11] http://somalbanca.org/financial-institutions/brief-history-of-the-somali-financial-institutions.html. Brief History of the Somali Financial Institutions. Central Bank of Somalia.
[12] 20 http://somalbanca.org/financial-institutions/brief-history-of-the-somali-financial-institutions.html. Brief History of the Somali Financial Institutions. Central Bank of Somalia.

confidence in the local currency some of which are counterfeits. Dollarization notwithstanding, the large issuance of the Somali shilling increasingly fuels price rises, especially for the low value transactions to the extent that inflation runs in high double digits and the Somali shilling is continuously on a depreciation trend. The inflationary environment is expected to cease as soon as the Central Bank takes full charge of monetary policy and replaces the presently circulating currency printed by the private sector."[13]

Despite such determined and hopeful rhetoric, these efforts have largely been frustrated. The transitional government sacked its governor in 2005 for disobeying orders, and the governor protested that its action was illegal and unconstitutional. In its current state, the central bank cannot control the money supply, particularly since the country has largely been dollarized, and has no monetary policy or interest rate setting ability.

In the south there have long been plans to reactivate the Central Bank of Somalia and to issue bank notes through it. However, in the absence of a centralized government, there has been little to stop other economic agents from importing bank notes. The prospect of the Central Bank performing a leading role in the economy is remote for several years at least.[14] Even then the resumption of exercising monetary policy by the Central Bank is however handicapped by lack of adequate resources, both financial and material. . Somalia is one of only four members of the Arab League that does not belong to the Arab Bank of Economic Development in Africa (ABEDA).

Despite Somaliland utilising its own currency; alongside the Somali shilling, the US dollar is generally widely accepted as a medium of large and high transactions even for local trade exchanges. The economy is deeply dollarized in view of weak confidence in the local currency some of which are counterfeits; dollarization notwithstanding, the large issuance of the Somali shilling increasingly fuels price rises especially for the low value transactions to the extent that inflation runs in high double digits and the Somali shilling is continuously on a depreciation trend. The inflationary environment is expected to stabilise providing that the Central Bank takes full charge of monetary policy and

---

[13] http://somalbanca.org/. The Central Bank of Somalia. Monetary Policy
[14] EIU. www.eiu.com. Somalia Country Profile 2008. Economic Intelligence Unit

issues a new currency and develops its institutional strengths and basis.

The Central Bank of Somalia's medium and longer term monetary policy objectives are:

- **Price stability**
- **Formulating and implementing monetary and exchange rate policies**
- **Maintaining and enhancing the value of the Somali Shilling**
- **Maintaining financial stability**
- **Harmonizing and coordinating government fiscal**
- **policies with monetary policies**[15]

Somaliland & Puntland Bank Developments: In the northern self-declared state of Somaliland; the Central Bank of Somaliland, which also provides some commercial banking services, has been established, but no other formal financial institutions exist. The Somaliland Central Bank prints and dispenses its own currency the Somaliland Shilling which like the region is unrecognised and this has perhaps acted as the biggest impediment to Somaliland's relatively steady banking system. However, the exception is Dahabshiil, which has its headquarters in Hargeisa and has recently introduced a debit card along with ATMs in Hargeisa as well as the Dahabshiil Bank. In addition, Somaliland's parliament passed "The Banking Law" in 2012 as well as the "Islamic Banking Law" which was a landmark piece of legislation and opened the door for foreign banks to enter. According to reports; Yemeni state-owned bank CAC, Djibouti-based Salaam African Bank, and Banque de Depot de Credit Djibouti, a subsidiary of Switzerland-headquartered Swiss Financial Investments, have all approached the regions authorities about commencing operations in Somaliland.[16]

The Central Bank of Puntland became operational in Bosaso in August 1999[17] and has also adopted a monetary policy as its framework. Indeed, Puntland's Central Bank is enshrined in its constitution, however, similar to the Somaliland Central Bank it

---

[15] http://www.centralbank.so
[16] http://www.reuters.com/article/2012/04/23/somalia-somaliland-banks-idAFL5E8FN8T720120423
[17] www.eiu.com. Somalia Country Profile 2008. Economic Intelligence Unit.

too has had problems attracting liquidity and general assets. In this respect it provides basic commercial services for mainly salaried state employees such as; civil servants, soldiers and teachers.

Public Finance Management Policy: More recently, the Somali government has endorsed a new Public Finance Management Policy (PFMP). The policy, announced in May, 2013, is a positive sign of the continued progress being made within Somalia's financial sector. After the policy was approved by the cabinet, Prime Minister Abdi Farah Shirdon stated:
"We have endorsed the reform plan as the guiding principle of public financial management and re-establishing Somali institutions." *He added:* "The plan envisages an impressive reform agenda in public finance management."
The PFMP was designed to improve the government's financial sector delivery capability and provide timely, transparent and accurate financial information across the public sector. An official press release stated that the Somali government was committed to ensuring the full implementation of the plan over the next four years. Indeed, the government has expressed a sense of urgency in undertaking these financial reforms. Further explanations of the government policy on PFMP pointed out that the step taken was in support of service delivery to improve transparency and openness in the national budget. The Cabinet underlined that it aims to enhance fiscal discipline through internal and external control. "It (PFMP) also enhances efficiency and effectiveness of public expenditure and puts the focus of public expenditure on government priority areas," stated the government document.

According to the Federal Government's Finance and Planning minister Mohamud Hassan Suleiman, the implementation of the reform plan will cost $26 million, over the four years term of his government. This development comes at a time Somalia was attempting to re-establish links with other governments, financial partners. Global Institutions and re-assert itself on the world stage. Incidentally, the Somaliland administration with support from DFID and the World Bank adopted a Public Financial Management policy in early 2011.[18]

---

[18] http://somalilandpress.com/somaliland-launches-public-financial-management-reforms-20712

Somali Stock Exchange

Founded in March 2011, the Somali Stock Exchange (SSE) was launched by the Somali Economic Forum (SEF) in September, 2015.
The SSE was established to attract investment from both Somali-owned firms and global companies, in order to speed-up the post-conflict reconstruction process in Somalia.

The SSE signed a Memorandum of Understanding with the Nairobi Securities Exchange (NSE) to assist it in technical development. The agreement includes the identification of appropriate expertise and support.

In November 2015, the Somali Stock Exchange established administrative offices in Mogadishu, Hargeisa, and other urban centres in Somalia. It also set-up a bureau in Nairobi, staffed by Somali stockbrokers and trained staff.

On the 1st of September, 2015, the Somali Stock Exchange (SSE) began selling its first shares at the Exchange's headquarters in Garowe, Somalia. The SEE also held its first conference at the Puntland Chambers of Commerce in Bosaso, during its launch.

The Somali Stock Exchange made history by becoming the first ever stock exchange to operate inside Somalia!

The demand for capital is increasing by the day for Somali businesses and liquidity is key, as in any market across the world. According to latest statistics, over 3 billion USD flows in to Somali every year – and a large stake of that cash is for businesses.

The Somali Stock Exchange is one of many examples of Somalia's changing fortunes. The SSE is projected to grow from strength to strength, as there is a substantial capital pool available to the Somali diaspora. Previously, these diaspora investors would be forced to invest their capital in other markets, such as Nairobi or Dubai. However, with the emergence of the first Somali Stock Exchange, they can now invest and seek capital investment within Somalia's own borders and main urban centres.

Over 20 firms are already listed on the SSE and it aims to attract even more firms in the near future.

It is believed that the Somali Stock Exchange will truly allow Somalis to live up to their commercial reputation as traders and business people; thereby connecting Somalis across the world.

The SSE **Vision** is far ranging: to be an excellent, Somalia-based stock exchange and the premier capital market in the Horn of Africa / East African Region – which will best serve its stakeholders and partners.

The SSE **Mission** is to develop a high quality market and exchange for its Somali and international investors.

SSE **Aims** to serve and empower its customers by providing world-class market technology, innovative products and solutions, as well as a fair and efficient market.

An Initial Public Offering (IPO), provides firms with the opportunity to make shares of a company liquid, thereby paying dividends to shareholders. Many investors invest only in listed companies, simply due to the fact that listed companies are subject to stricter requirements and greater scrutiny. For potential investors, this inspires greater confidence.

With offices in large commercial Somali cities such as: Garowe, Bosaso, Hargeisa and Mogadishu, the Somali Stock Exchange (SSE) is the only exchange that can meet the needs of investor and firms from diverse sectors. The SSE also caters to Blue Chip firms and large companies that do not wish to be listed publicly on a regulated market.

Established companies, SME's, start-up companies and issuers of Equity certificates can be listed on the SSE. The admission requirements to the SSE are less comprehensive or cumbersome than the requirements of exchanges abroad, with a relatively swift and efficient process. One early adopter was the Somali Postal Express, a logistics company that was formed in January 2015.

Benefits of an SSE Listing:

- **Improving a company's capital raising capabilities, which can be used for sustained growth or to fund acquisitions / investments in key sectors.**
- **Attract skilled professionals and investors from the extensive Somali Diaspora and international investors who are easily able to trade in SSE-listed shares, without any restrictions.**
- **Market businesses to investors with the assistance of the SSE Business Development Team.**
- **Enhance relations with key stakeholders such as banks, foreign investors and industry leaders.**
- **Receive a market valuation of the company.**
- **Listing on the SSE is an assurance quality stamp of approval.**
- **Access to the member firms that trade on the SSE.**
- **Detailed market surveillance and active monitoring of each company.**
- **The SSE publishes Annual reports and half-yearly interim reports.**

3. Remittances

The coordination of remittances - or wealth transfers from abroad - is a well-established practice in Somalia. Remittances are closely linked to Somalia's role since the 1970s as a labour reserve for Gulf States and (since the mid-1980s) as a diaspora community in the West.

In the 1970s and 1980s, the most common means of remitting wealth was called the 'franco valuta' system. Somali migrant labourers flocking to high-paying jobs in the Gulf either purchased high value consumer goods and shipped them back to family members, or transferred their salaries via Somali traders, who then paid their relatives in Somali shillings and used the hard currency to purchase imports[19]. Whilst this rudimentary system of remittances was rather on the primitive side, it swiftly developed into an important pillar of the Somali economy, to such an extent that researchers in a 1983 study found that, far from being a "brain drain" Somalia's export of its own labour was the most efficient utilisation of the workforce - earning higher value abroad than at home[20].

Since the collapse of the Somali central government and state financial institutions in the 1990s, Somalia has become even more reliant on money transfers from family members working abroad.

This absence of financial institution (i.e. licensed commercial banks) has seen remittance companies fill the void and evolve into informal financial institutions, most of which provide banking services on a nationwide basis.

Today, remittances are undoubtedly the largest single source of hard currency entering the Country, and are of vital significance with regards to the Country's ability to function effectively and develop its economy.

It is estimated that Somali money transfer organisations (MTO's) handle more than £1.3 billion in remittances on an annual basis and considerable more in commercial trade[21]. A noteworthy facet of the £1.3 billion Somali migrants around the World back to friends and families at home is the fact that it dwarfs humanitarian aid to Somalia[22].

---

[19] Ken Menkhaus. Remittance Companies and Money Transfers in Somalia. October 2001

[20] Boston University, African Studies Center, The Somali Social and Institutional Profile: An Executive Summary (Boston: Boston University, 1983), African Studies Center Working Paper No. 79. See also Norman Miller, "The Other Somalia: Illicit Trade and the Hidden Economy." Horn of Africa 5, 3 (1982), 3-19.

[21] Orozco, M. Yansura, J. (2013). Keeping the Lifeline Open. [Online] Available: http://www.oxfam.org/en/policy/keeping-somalia-lifeline-open.

[22] Orozco, M. Yansura, J. (2013). Keeping the Lifeline Open. [Online] Available: http://www.oxfam.org/en/policy/keeping-somalia-lifeline-open.

Remittance Companies Operating in Somalia

Dahabshiil	Qaran Express	Olympic
Amal Express	Kaah Express	Hodan Global
Amana Express	Iftin Express	Tawakal Express
World Remit	Western Union	Jubba Express
Olympic	Mustaqbal	Medina

The successful growth of remittance companies in Somalia is almost completely dependent on social capital – namely the cohesiveness and trust within communities. Had it not been for the existence of this social capital and the safe "Hawala" system of financial transfers across continents, perhaps the rapid growth in capital investment, commerce and trade would not have transpired.

Today, there are more than 17 MTO's in the industry including the international giant Western Union.

Studies of remittances in Hargeisa, Burco and Bosasso calculated that remittances constitute nearly 40 percent of the income of urban households, which would leave roughly 14 percent for average rural consumption[23].

Besides direct re-distributions, there are also spill-over effects. A study in Hargeisa found that usually those, who earn less than $2/day, have no direct access to remittances from abroad but have to rely on gifts from family members or neighbours.

---

[23] Gundel, J. (2003). "The Migration-Development Nexus: Somalia Case Study". In Van Hear, N. and Nyberg Sørensen, N. (eds) The Migration-Development Nexus. Geneva: IOM.

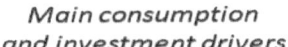
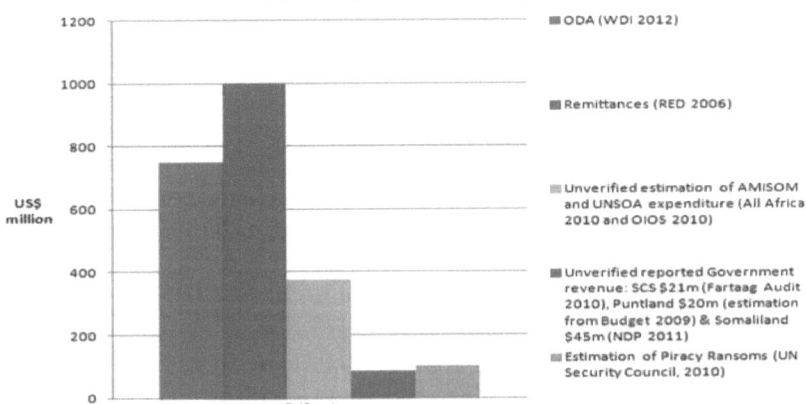

One negative impact is that remittances might discourage job-seeking and keep unemployment high.

In terms of the demographic breakdown of those that remit, over £160 million comes from the United Kingdom, with the Somali diaspora in the: US, Western European and Middle Eastern countries generally making up the other significant remittance contributions.

Individual transfers are usually less than £200 and are depended on by families for basic costs such as food, water, education, healthcare and so forth. A recent report by the UN Food and Agricultural Organisation shows that up to 40 percent of families in Somaliland and Puntland receive some form of remittance, and that the money is integral to their survival[24].

Apart from the vital small amounts of money sent by relatives from the diaspora, the remittance services provided by money transfer companies contribute to investments, commerce and reconstruction projects across Somalia new organisations and development projects (Hansen, 2003). In the absence of internationally recognised banks; these remittance companies are considered as reliable and trustworthy as 'local Banks' They provide some of the facilities offered by conventional Banks, such as saving and current accounts to individuals, private companies and international organisations, thus facilitating international

---

[24] FAO. (2013). Remittances and Livelihoods Support in Puntland and Somaliland. Available: http://www.fsnau.org/downloads/Remittances-and-Livelihoods-Sup- port-in-Puntland-and-Somaliland.pdf

payments for imports. In addition to the key roles that remittance companies play in the economic development of the Country in terms of trade, investment and livelihood security, they are also among the leading private sector employers in Somalia.

While remittance money represents an imperative segment of the Somali economy, there is scarce amount of accurate information about the actual volume of the cash flow transiting through money transfer companies. However, according to estimated calculations, the amount of remittance that flows into Somaliland alone (which is home to 1/5 of the Somalia's total population) could be in the region of US$780 Million annually. About 30% of this ($234 Million) comes in as capital and/or financial investments and the remaining 70% ($546 Million) comes in as small money between $100 and $500, received as household maintenance for families and individuals. Another study calculates that remittances constitute nearly 40% of the income of urban households in the northern towns of Hargeisa, Burao, and Bosasso[25]. In light of the aforementioned figures, it is without doubt that the remittance sector is by far the biggest contributor to Somaliland's economy (i.e. 54% of the country's GDP). Considering this is the case for Somaliland alone, it is without doubt that the size and scope of the remittance sector is far greater when you take into account the rest of (South Central) Somalia. Even if remittances to southern Somalia are less well-documented, it is known that Mogadishu is unquestionably the largest recipient of remittances; it probably accrues a similar level of remittances as does Somaliland. In the town of Beled Weyn, with a population of about 50,000, an estimated US$200,000 per month is received in remittances, for a monthly average of US$4 per town dweller.[26]

Whether invested or consumed, remittances have important macroeconomic impacts. They generate positive multiplier effects in local communities, indirectly benefiting households, which do not receive remittances themselves, while also stimulating various sectors of the economy. Researchers have found that for every dollar a developing nation receives from migrants working abroad,

---

[25] Khalid Medani, "Report on Migration and Remittance Inflows: Northwest and Northeast Somalia." Nairobi: UNCU and FSAU, 2000.
[26] Ken Menkhaus, "Hiran Region," UNDOS Studies on Governance, (2000).

the GNP rose by $ 2.69 to 3.17 depending on whether remittances were received by urban or rural households27.

An emerging trend is that while remittances were - throughout most of the 1990s - used to finance purchases of basic consumer goods, in recent years there has been a shift toward use of remittance money by more middle-class families for investment purposes – mainly in real estate, but also in small businesses.28

4. Regulation

As discussed throughout this report, Somalia has only recently seen the emergence of a nascent, formal banking sector. Therefore, it is no surprise that Somalia's regulatory framework is rudimentary in regards to banking and finance activities.

The past two years have witnessed not only the international recognition of the Federal Government of Somalia, but also the increased level of funding pledged by donor states at the Brussels Conference in 2013. Indeed, this is all significant, as a key focus of international engagement with Somalia's government has been increasing regulation and transparency. Central to this has been the focus on institutional support to Somalia's Central Bank, which has been empowered in the past two years with increased training for officials and increased capacity building. The aim is to provide the Central Bank with the necessary support to enable it to act as a key regulatory body within the country, granting commercial banking licences and dispensing accredited currency. However, for this to happen, there will need to be a considerable and focused investment in Somali government institutions such as the Central Bank which will enable a healthy regulatory environment to emerge in Somalia. Also, prior to this, there needs to be the right legislation enacted to ensure that the Central Bank is provided with the necessary legal capital to fulfil its mandate.

In the case of Somaliland, a Banking Law was passed in 2012 and progress in commercial banking has been gradual at best. Yet, this has still enabled the Somaliland Central Bank and government to adopt basic regulatory mechanisms such as an internal auditing

---

[27] Maimbo, S.M. (2006) Remittances and Economic Development in Somalia. Social development papers, conflict prevention and reconstruction paper No.38

[28] Kulaksiz and Purdekova (2006); Somali remittance sector: a macroeconomic perspective. Social development papers, conflict prevention and reconstruction paper No.38

department within the bank, which oversees its activities. However, it is important to note that the Federal Government of Somalia has employed the international, financial firm PriceWaterhouseCoopers to act as an auditor of the Central Bank and various government institutions.

Indeed, it is crucial that the central government of Somalia formulates and implements various regulatory mechanisms and a regulatory framework, as this will prevent excessive oversights and inefficient banks from operating. With the current declaration by the Somali government that they intend to entice foreign, commercial banks, then it is even more of a pressing issue for the regulatory framework to be established - this will prevent predatory banks from entering the market.

5. Mobile Banking

Mobile banking refers to financial services delivered via mobile networks and performed on a mobile (cell) phone. Indeed, economists have noted the rise in mobile banking innovation in East Africa with the dominance of M-Pesa in Kenya and Zaad within Somalia.

Zaad is a mobile banking service provided to major Somali telecommunication firms such as: Telesom and Hormuud Telecom and acts as the dominant money transfer system. Zaad has picked up more than 300,000 users since its launch three years ago through the Telesom network. Payments and transactions are made which are incredibly efficient and secure, enabling parents to send money to children at school or employers to pay their employees[29]. On average, single customers are limited to transfers of $500, while accredited merchants can move up to $2,000. Most private sector businesses use the system and Telesom pays all of its employees using Zaad.

Mobile Banking is increasingly becoming more popular with both regional Somali banks due to a wide array of factors, most notably the advantage of drastically cutting down the costs of providing service to the customers. For example an average teller or phone transaction costs about is $1 each, whereas an electronic transaction costs only about $0.10 each. Additionally, this new

---

[29] http://www.theglobeandmail.com/news/world/how-mobile-phones-are-making-cash-obsolete-in-africa/article12756675/

channel gives the bank the ability to advertise and up-sell their other banking products, which is a technique already adopted by Somali Mobile banking providers like Hormuud, Telesom, Golis and Somalia Telecom. Moreover, Mobile Banking is more secure than many conventional ways of banking, due to the fact that it removes the necessity to carry cash – additionally, it is more secure than credit cards. Another reason why Mobile Banking is becoming increasingly popular is that it not only saves the client time, but also provides the added convenience allowing consumers to do their everyday banking, anytime, anywhere - as long as they are connected to the Internet.

Fig 2.3: African Mobile Connection & Penetration Rate

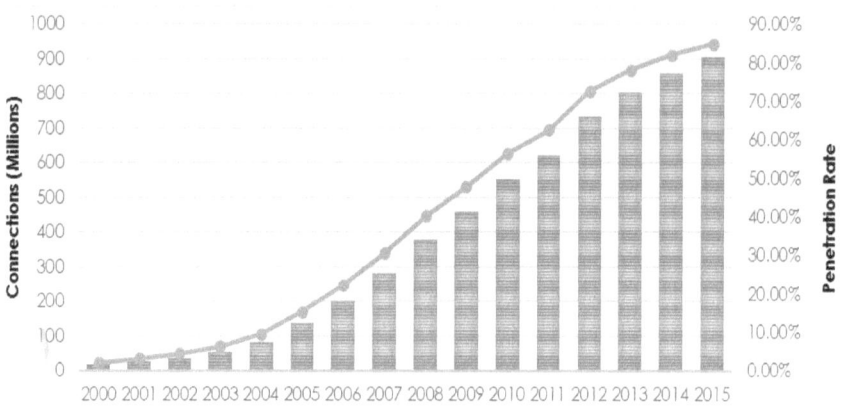

The graph above displays the mobile connection and penetration rate on the African Continent and highlights the rapid rise in both mobile connections as well as penetration rates, with the later showing exponential growth from 2005 onwards. The forecasts suggest the trend will continue and indicates Mobile phones will become integral to the lives of Africans across the continent.

There is forecast a huge jump in terms of mobile phone payments between 2012 and 2016. We've already seen companies like Starbucks adopt mobile payment, but it is assumed that in the next couple of years it will reach the tipping point of adoption where the majority of early adopters and early majority are using this technology.

617b is forecast to be paid via mobile transactions with 418m users by 2016. Africa and Asia will account for a staggering 60% of all such mobile payments.

In 2012, the Bill & Melinda Gates Foundation, the World Bank and the Gallup World Poll found that one-third of adults in Somalia had used mobile money. Furthermore, the 2012 MMU Global Mobile Money Adoption Survey revealed that Somalia had one of the world's highest rates of customer uptake. The World Bank's Global Financial Inclusion Database (Findex) recently revealed that Somalia was one of the most active mobile money markets:

26% of the population reported using mobiles to pay bills, which is the highest rate in the World, and 32% to send and receive money. Most of this mobile money activity has been driven by Telesom ZAAD. In early 2009, Telesom ZAAD succeeded in becoming the 5th telecommunication company in the world that provides MMT (mobile money transfer) technology to its customers, a remarkable achievement.

It is evident that the Somali market is very receptive to mobile-based services and applications, as well as underlining the increasing Somali market and utilisation of mobile phone services. Mobile transactions occur predominantly through Sahal, EMAAL and Telesom Zaad.

These service providers receive a high volume of transactions, averaging around 34 transactions per customer on a regular weekly basis. These services were introduced in 2009 and now total 14 - with Sahal, EMAAL and Telesom Zaad at the forefront. Since their inception in 2009, limited innovation has taken place, and most of the mobile payment services are SMS-based catering for feature phones.

According to some of the figures released by Samsung, 1 in 15 phones shipped are smartphones, this is predicted to increase to 1 in 5 or 6 in 2015. Given how integral mobile devices are in the horn of Africa, services and products developed by banks in this region need to have a strong mobile strategy to cater for customer behaviours and usage patterns.

In general, the banking sector in Somalia currently comprises of an active informal sector and virtually non-existent formal sector. The private sector remittance companies dominate the informal sector, whereas the formal banking sector includes central banks in Mogadishu (southern Somalia), Hargeysa (Somaliland) and Bosasso (Puntland).

6. Economic Opportunities and Investments

The recent revival of Somalia as a regional and international player has enabled it to attract considerable inward investment from its large diaspora and the increased availability of finance funds, along with a rise in demand for financing from Somali banks. With the importance of remittances within Somalia, coupled with its large diaspora, it is imperative to note that this has enabled inward investment and increased demand for finance within various sectors such as: hospitality, telecommunications and property etc. This rise in investment has been mostly felt in Mogadishu, which has undergone intense reconstruction and development within the last year, mainly due to increased air network links, which have facilitated the rise in diaspora returnees.

In addition, this investment has not just been monetary but also through skilled labour transfer which has also been facilitated by UN agencies[30]. Such increased inward investment has enabled members of the diaspora to open various SMEs and ventures, which have had a multiplier effect: further jobs are created and the economy is buoyed. However, this increased investment has only been possible thanks to the increase in the availability of finance funds and increased consumer activity amongst households in Somalia. A major problem currently exists which will only be exacerbated in the coming years, which is the lack of loans available to finance investment. The ever-expanding diaspora middle-class have a high demand for loans to finance their financial pursuits such as: buying property and investing in the expanding real estate sector. Somali banks do not yet possess enough capacity to provide loans to the business community or middle classes. Nevertheless, this increased financial investment of the diaspora and middle-class in Somalia conveys the lucrative and significant market that the banking sector faces in Somalia.

When looking at finance and banking in Somalia, Foreign Direct Investment (FDI) can act as an indicator to look at the ever-expanding market for finance and banking. For example, various African banks have stated their interest to penetrate the Somali market and, in particular, Iman Bank (a subsidiary of a major Kenyan bank) and this has made inroads in investing in Somalia, due to its significant potential. The rise of FDI in Somalia has enabled increased finance opportunities for foreign banks and there has been much discussion amongst various banks that have an eye on investing in the Somali banking sector.

Economists have long claimed that Somalia provides the perfect foundation to become a major banking hub in the region, due to the primacy of the private sector and the entrepreneurial nature of Somalis. Foreign banks that venture into Somalia whilst the formal banking sector is in its infancy, will benefit considerably in

---

[30] http://www.quests-mida.org/

the long run as this is a sector that will explode in coming years. It is no surprise to see various remittance firms restructuring themselves as banks - they are all too aware that their solid consumer base - diaspora adults - will be replaced by second generation Somalis who will feel less inclined to send money back to relatives in Somalia. As a result of this generational shift, they have focused on strengthening their banking activities, which they believe will act as the next frontier in Somalia's economic development.

7. Summary

Somalia's private sector has done surprisingly well, as it is not only surviving, but growing in conditions of a free-market, supported by steady remittance flows. Even so, there are pitfalls to a post-conflict economy without a proper functioning central bank and financial institutions; the most important being failure to provide public goods and to correct negative externalities. Although it is true that the private sector and the NGOs picked up the provision of key services after the "exit" of the state from this arena, this provision has been extremely narrow in scope.

While remittances play an important role in the Somali economy, they cannot become a source of long-term sustainable growth. In the medium term, if there is an improvement in the political and security situation, it is expected that part of former remittances will turn into domestically-sourced investment, as Somalis start returning home. In the longer term, regulations need to be put in place to promote investment, which is a crucial pre-condition for long-term economic growth.

CHAPTER THREE

TELECOMMUNICATIONS AND ECONOMIC POLICIES

Introduction:

One of the main objectives of the Somali Economic Forum has always been to promote sustainable economic development in Somalia and, central to this, is the development of Somalia's financial sector.

Somalis are an oral people by their nature and, as a result, a robust and vibrant telecommunications sector will prove to be crucial in terms of fostering rapid economic growth and development.

Indeed, the mobile telecommunications industry in Somalia has grown rapidly over the last two decades, representing one of the most intriguing stories of technology diffusion in Africa.

1. Overview of the Telecommunications Sector in Somalia

For a country that until recently did not even have an effective central government, Somalia has an amazingly well developed and sophisticated telecommunications sector, with a healthy amount of competition. Prior to the overthrow of Siad Barre's Socialist regime in 1991, the telecommunications sector in Somalia had always been in the public domain, which saw the domination of powerful state-owned telecom operators with set prices, heavy regulation and limited services.

However, in the aftermath of the collapse of the central government, the then dormant private sector has exploded and perhaps the biggest beneficiary of this private sector dominance has been the telecommunications sector. Indeed, following the 1991 outbreak of the war; the chaos at the time led to the destruction of the Public Switch Transmission Network and other key telecommunications infrastructure, which served to provide communication services for the majority of urban residents. Hence, for a number of years the country's telecommunication network was destroyed and disconnected from the rest of the world. Therefore, Somalis were generally without the means to connect to the large expatriate community of friends and relatives outside the country, and, vice versa. However, for business-savvy Somali entrepreneurs, this void in the market presented an opportunity rather than a dilemma. In the next 20 years, these Somali businessmen and investors successfully exploited the gap in an unregulated market of various privately-owned companies, which had emerged in the 1990s and early 2000s. These telecommunication firms then competed to provide the populace with key telecommunications infrastructure and services, both at the local and international level. In 1993 alone, nine telecommunication companies emerged.

With the privatisation of these companies, came intense competition, allowing for an expansion of mobile services, greater efficiency and crucially an overall decrease in prices, which basic economics tells us always occurs due to competition. Importantly, this intense competition also led to significant technological advancements in the sector and, even today, Somalia's telecommunications sector is by far the most innovative and technological receptive sector within its economy.

This telecommunications boom also sparked the creation of the Somali Telecom Association (STA), signed by roughly ten Somali operators, along with the International Telecommunication Union (ITU) and United Nations Development Programme (UNDP) Somalia, which was signed in 1998.

In the current unregulated economy, the telecommunication sector has flourished, facilitated by the lack of barriers to entry and the simplicity of the infrastructure required. This sector has also been buoyed by the substantial and consistent rise in mobile and Internet usage amongst the Somali population, as well as the potential high and quick returns investors can make from their investment in the telecommunications sector.

Together with the remittances system, telecommunications has become the leading private sector industry in Somalia[31]. Analysts

---

[31] ITU (Bannon, I., Hahn, S. and Schwartz, J. (2004) 'The Private Sector's Role in the Provision of Infrastructure in Post-conflict Countries: Patterns and Policy Options' Conflict Prevention and Reconstruction No. 16 (Washington DC, US: World Bank).

believe that Somalia has some of the best telecommunications systems in Africa, with a number of companies even offering competitive data and voice services. Indeed, according to The Economist, Somalia benefits from the cheapest calling rates in Africa and by extension the world.[32] In the aftermath of the civil war in the early 1990s, Somalia's telecommunications companies have expanded and thrived in an unregulated environment.

1.1 Growth of the Telecommunications Sector

The rapid development of technology in Somalia comes as numerous telecommunication providers and firms compete in a deregulated and lucrative market with the absence of: taxes, red tape, the collapse of foreign exchange controls and the absence of license providers and state controlled telecommunications firms to crowd out the market.
Telecom operators have moved quickly to take advantage of the lack of restrictions and regulations made possible by the lack of a strong, functioning central government in the past 20 years. This conducive environment also allowed telecommunications infrastructure and equipment to be brought in cheaply and easily. The aforementioned reasons are perhaps the most notable contributing factors, enabling Somalia's various telecommunication firms to become among the most sophisticated and innovative in East Africa, meaning that consumers can make the cheapest local and international calling rates in the world.

It is important for observers of Somalia's telecommunications sector to note that, prior to the explosion in mobile usage, Somalia benefited from a high usage of landline telecommunications. Yet, such has been the development in mobile phones in Africa that customers in Somalia can now conduct money transfers and other banking activities via mobile phones, as well as utilise wireless access.

There are presently over 20 telecom companies in Somalia and around 25 mainlines per 1,000 persons, and the local availability of telephone lines (tele-density) is higher than in neighbouring countries and three times greater than in adjacent Ethiopia[33].

---

[32] http://www.economist.com/node/5328015
[33] World Bank/UNDP (2002) Somali Socio-Economic Survey 2011 (Washington DC, US: World Bank).

Figure 3.1: Growth of Phone Lines (1991 – 2002)

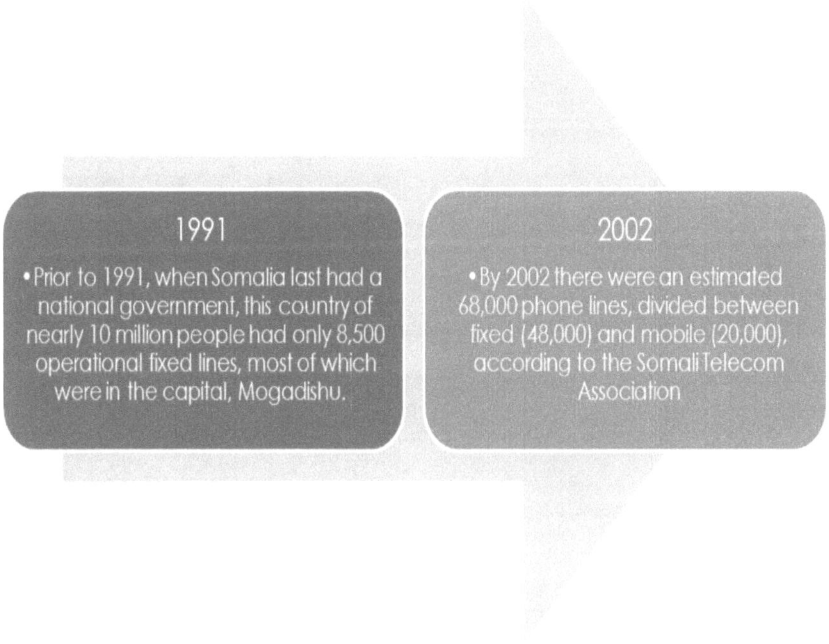

1991
- Prior to 1991, when Somalia last had a national government, this country of nearly 10 million people had only 8,500 operational fixed lines, most of which were in the capital, Mogadishu.

2002
- By 2002 there were an estimated 68,000 phone lines, divided between fixed (48,000) and mobile (20,000), according to the Somali Telecom Association

2. Market size and key players

The main telecommunication networks in Somalia are shown in the diagram below:

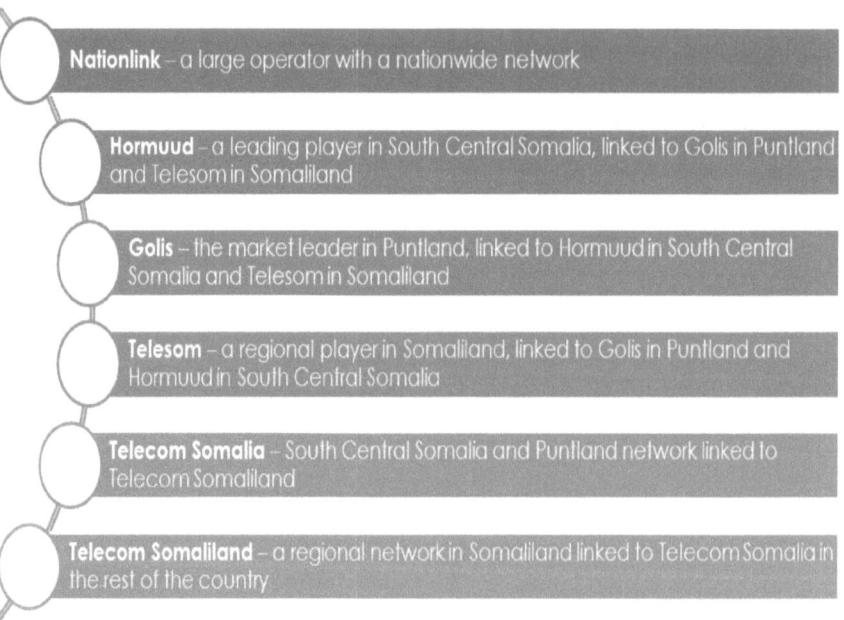

The main problem hindering Somalia's telecommunications sector is poor interconnectivity between the different mobile phone networks. This is particularly serious in South Central Somalia. Essentially this means that users of one mobile network cannot call friends or relatives who use another mobile network. Somalia's telecommunications firms follow this policy to try capture consumers and hinder their competitors. As a result of this policy, Somali consumers have no choice but to carry two SIM cards. Such an issue is unheard of in developed states and this is mainly down to the existence of a central government and regulatory bodies to stop such private sector excesses. Another issue is that the lack of radio spectrum control has led to harmful interference between the signals of rival networks in some areas. Many Somalis resort to using several different SIM cards (and phone numbers) to get round this problem and many have mobile phones that can take up two or three different SIM cards. However, Somali telecommunication firms have made an effort to combat such practices, for example: Hormuud, Golis and Telecom do have good connectivity with each other, after making a tripartite agreement. This has enabled customers to make calls between networks and gain access to a much larger network area. In order to achieve this, the managers of the three companies created a multi-company technical committee to study the possibility of implementing inter-operability. They succeeded and went ahead with the implementation. Now, the initiator of the call takes $0.08 a minute, while the receiver gets $0.07 cents a minute[34]. The fact that all three companies are partly owned by Ahmed Nur Ali Jimale, the former boss of the Al Barakat money transfer company, has made this interconnectivity much easier as the spectre of competition is removed.

Puntland has fairly good and extensive mobile network coverage. Some companies have extended their range in Puntland, especially the urban regions around: Bossasso, Galkayo, Qardho and Garowe, which all have good mobile coverage. Yet, some remote and mountainous areas are out of range due to a lack of telecommunication infrastructure. Somaliland still suffers problems of connectivity between its different mobile networks that all compete with one another fiercely, but since 2000, the Somaliland Association of Telecom Operators has been in operation. It has helped to tackle this issue of the lack of interconnectivity. A Memorandum of Understanding was signed by seven major telecommunications companies and the Association is helping to bring about a more cohesive and sophisticated development of the telecommunications sector in Somaliland.

It is important to remember that the make-up of the telecommunications sector and the major players in Somalia is distinct to most other developing states in Africa and elsewhere. The main reason is that in most other states; it is state-owned, public telecommunication providers that usually dominate this sector with a near monopoly which is usually safeguarded by the government. However, in Somalia this has not occurred due to the lack of a strong central government in the past 20 years and regional governments with a limited reach. This has then led to the situation in Somalia whereby powerful private telecommunication

---

[34] Yusuf, A. (2006). Somali Enterprises: Making Peace their Business. International Alert. P474 – 508. London, UK.

firms exist with a near monopoly in the regions that they operate and dominate within Somalia.

With over 10 years of experience and an excellent record of expansion, Hormuud continues to be the market leader with over 60% of market share in both mobile and broadband services[35]. However, given the dynamic nature of the sector, with its rapid rate of mergers, closures and start-ups, it is difficult to quantify the exact size of the market or the number of people employed. However, the following description (i.e. 1.5) of, 'The Industry Leader and Other Key Players', gives some indication of the sector's size, capacity and major operators.

Hormuud Telecom (Hortel): The largest telecommunication firm in all regions across Somalia is Hormuud Telecom Somali Inc (Hortel), which was formed in 2002 and has since grown to become the industry leader in telecommunication the horn of Africa nation. Headquartered in Mogadishu, Hormuud has sales surpassing $40 million a year. Contextualized with the fact that 70% of the country lives on less than $2 a day, Hormuud is one of the most economically prosperous companies in Somalia[36]. As an industry leader, Hormuud has 3000 investors in general, 600 of which are shareholders, this set up proved to be a wise decision by the board of directors, as it has enabled Hormuud to have the funds to sustain their growth and allocate resources where appropriate. The company now directly employs 6,000 employees and a further 15,000 indirectly and that makes Hormuud the largest employer in Somalia; providing a livelihood to more than 150,000 Somalis[37].

For the past decade, companies like Hormuud have been offering reliable telephone services with affordable local and international calls often serving the even the remotest villages in the country.

---

[35] Anon, A. (2010). Hormuud Telecom. Available: http://www.hortel.net/viewpage.php?page_id=1. [Accessed 6th Sep 2013]
[36] Farah, D. (2013). PennSID: Telecom Thrived Sans Governance. [Online] Available: http://www.pennsid.org/2013/02/telecom-thrived-sans-governance/. [Accessed 6th Sep 2013]
[37] Anon, A. (2010). Hormuud Telecom. Available: http://www.hortel.net/viewpage.php?page_id=1. [Accessed 6th Sep 2013]

Figure 3.3 – Hormuud Economic Impact Statistics

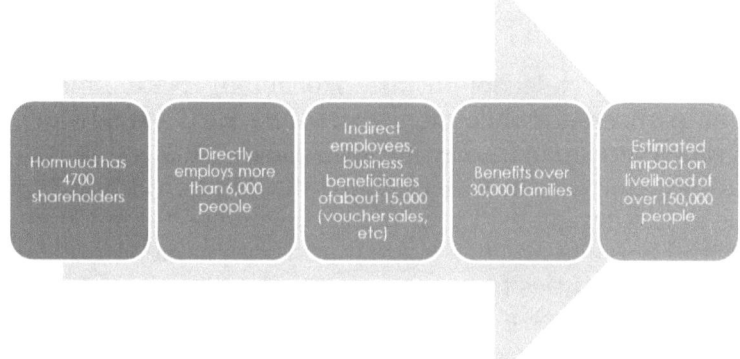

Moreover, Hormuud provides other value added services and is committed to providing innovative products, services and a culture that places high value on customer care.

Figure 3.4 – Value Added Services provided by Hormuud

The E-Voucher is an USSD-based credit transfer facility that enables all Hormuud customers to transfer credits from their account to any other Hormuud customer. This service replaces scratch-off cards, which are more costly to keep and may be more vulnerable to theft, thereby necessitating greater security precautions on the retailer's part. The E-voucher, by comparison, is a more secure and speedy method of transferring credit.

Somalia's major telecom firms: Hormuud, Nationlink and Telesom, pioneered mobile money transfers **EVC Plus**, which is an upgraded version of the E-voucher. Besides transferring cash to friends and relatives, the service allows one to pay utility bills and purchase everyday goods. The system is the first of its kind in south and central Somalia and has made it easy for people to trade and buy basic commodities from the market. The service requires the customer to complete a quick and free registration process and once consumers have registered for the EVC Plus, they can deposit cash with the mobile phone and send to other people signed up for the service at the click of a button. Moreover, EVC Plus reduces the security risks posed by carrying huge wads of the Somali currency around the open city markets, which would make traders prone to being robbed. Other benefits of EVC Plus is that the service works with all mobile phone models and customers don't have to stand in long queues to send money; finally, the service enables customers to send money to the furthest regions of Somalia without extra charges[38]

Hormuud International Postpaid Roaming Service enables Hormuud customers to make and receive calls as well as send and receive text messages while visiting another country. While travelling abroad, customers can rely on their Hormuud International Postpaid Roaming subscription to stay connected with friends, families and business associates. Hormuud's extensive International Roaming network covers over 300 Operators all over the world. Another benefit is that the service permits users to keep their same mobile number and service.

In December 2012, Hormuud made telecommunications history when it launched its Tri-Band 3G service for its mobile and Internet clients. This was a landmark achievement in Somalia as it was the first of its kind. When taken into consideration, the fact that the majority of mobile customers in the US and UK still utilise 3G then this achievement is even more astonishing. The potential

---

[38] Anon, A. (2010). Hormuud Telecom. Available: http://www.hortel.net/viewpage.php?page_id=1. [Accessed 6th Sep 2013]

of this 3G telecommunications technology is massive especially in terms of stimulating economic and business activity due to its faster and more secure connection. Also, in November 2013, Hormuud secured access to the new East African fibre optic link.

(Hormmud Telecom, Headquarters, Mogadishu.)

Golis Telecom Somalia (Golis) is the largest telecommunication operator in Puntland and the greater north-eastern region of Somalia. Founded in 2002 with the objective of supplying the country with GSM mobile services, fixed line and Internet services. Golis is headquartered in Bosaso, Puntland. Golis Telecom was created with the principal aim to provide Somalia with GSM mobile services, fixed line and Internet services. Above all, the Golis network coverage is so extensive that it generally covers all the major cities and more than 40 districts in both Puntland and Somaliland. According to The Economist, Golis has the amazing distinction of offering one of the cheapest international calling rates on the planet: at $0.20 USD, less than anywhere else in the entire world. The services provided by Golis Telecom generally vary and are diverse in nature. Golis does indeed offer innovative services such as its XOGMAAL service, which enables mobile consumers to surf the net, email through their mobile, and watch media on their phone. In recent years, Golis has stated its plan to roll out extensive 3G network coverage for all its consumers - a bold step. Golis Telecom has a binding agreement with two other companies namely Hormuud Telecom and Telesom. The three sister companies have set up a microwave system covering all Somalia and now every customer of Golis Telecom has access to make local calls to all Somalia from the southernmost point to the northernmost.

Telesom – Telesom is the main telecommunications firm in Somaliland and tends to dominate the market there. Its competitors includes Somtel (owned by Dahabshiil and SomCable). Telesom was established in 2001 and its services include; prepaid call plans, monthly subscription plans, International Roaming, MMS, WAP (over both GSM and GPRS), residential fixed line services, and broadband Internet plans. Telesom has gained a reputation as an innovator in the telecommunications sector within Somalia as it was one of the first firms to introduce 3G on July 3rd, 2011 which was almost 2 years earlier than some of its competitors.

It also provides 3G services to both prepaid and postpaid subscription customers. Telesom succeeded in enabling consumers to use social media sites such as Twitter and Facebook whilst offline, this strategic move by Telesom was announced during the 6th Somaliland Business Fair.[39]

This development coincided with the desire to entice younger consumers who will form the bulk of their future consumer base and who usually have a high percentage of mobile usage. In particular, Telesom has utilised the Zaad mobile banking services and benefited from increased consumer usage; substantially increasing its consumer base.

NationLink Telecom: Another major telecommunication firm is NationLink Telecom which was founded by Abdirizak Ido in the autumn of 1997. Headquartered in Mogadishu, the company provides telecommunication services all over Somalia and is one of the leading service providers in the country. The company's focus is in the core areas of: mobile, fixed lines, Internet and satellite mobile services. Nationlink is arguably the fastest expanding telecommunication firm in Somalia and increasingly provides services abroad, notably in the Democratic Republic of Congo, Rwanda and the Central African Republic[40].

3. Mobile Telecommunications and Mobile Banking

The mobile telecommunications industry in Somalia has grown rapidly over the last two decades, representing one of the most intriguing stories of technology diffusion in Africa. Since 2002, mobile subscribers have exceeded the number of fixed lines globally and this paradigm shift has been evident in Somalia for the past decade. The process to achieve what fixed phones have struggled for more than 120 years to do, took less than a fifth of the time for mobile networks. This crossover time of mobile users has been even shorter for developing countries. At the end of 2009, the number of mobile telecommunications subscribers reached 4.6 billion, which is equivalent to 67 per cent of the world population. This technology is particularly relevant in developing countries like Somalia, where there are more than twice as many subscriptions (3.2 billion) as in developed countries (1.4 billion)[41].

---

[39] http://somalilandpress.com/somalilandtelesom-unveils-new-customer-friendly-services-at-the-6th-somaliland-business-fair-47457

[40] Yusuf, A. (2006). Somali Enterprises: Making Peace their Business. *International Alert*. P474 – 508. London, UK.

[41] ITU (2005) World Telecommunication/ICT Development Report 2006: Measuring ICT for social and economic development. International Telecommunications Union, Geneva.

Figure 3.5: African Connection and Penetration Rates

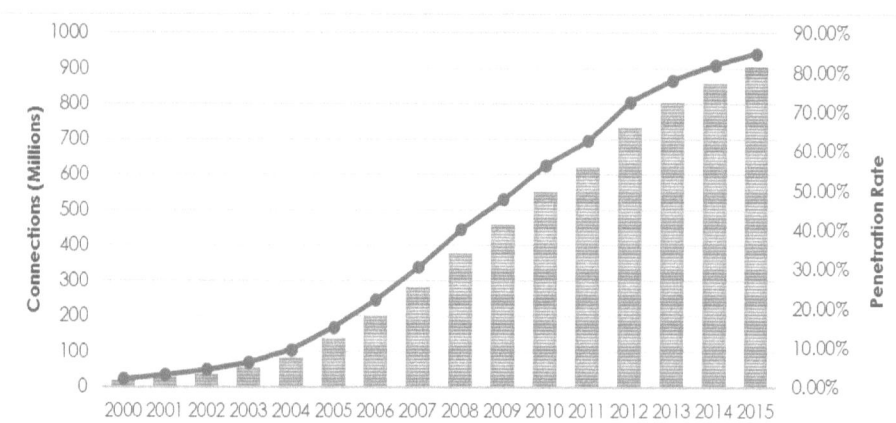

[GSMA, 2011]

The graph above displays the mobile connection and penetration rate on the African Continent and it highlights the rapid rise in both mobile connections as well as penetration rates, with the later showing exponential growth from 2005 onwards. The forecasts suggest the trend will continue and indicates mobile phones will become integral to the lives of Africans across the continent, especially the young who are becoming ever acquainted with mobile phones.

The importance of the telecommunications sector becomes also evident by comparing the share of telecommunications revenues in GDP: telecommunications services accounted for on average 4.8% of the total GDP of sub-Saharan Africa, compared to 3.1% in the European Union [42]. This alone tells us that the telecommunications sector in Africa is worth billions in potential

---

[42] United Nations Development Programme (UNDP) (2001) Human Development Report 2001: Making New Technologies Work for Human Development (New York, US: UNDP).

revenue and profit, as it captures such a large segment of economic activity.

While the conventional telecommunication sector brings about many economic benefits to developing countries like Somalia, these positive economic impacts are exceeded by the mobile telecommunication sub-sector. This is due to lower access cost to the user, compared to wired telecommunications. This technology could reach completely new segments of population particularly in developing countries, as is already evident in Somalia and across East Africa (See Fig 3.6)

Figure 3.6: Number of registered and active mobile banking accounts by region (2012)

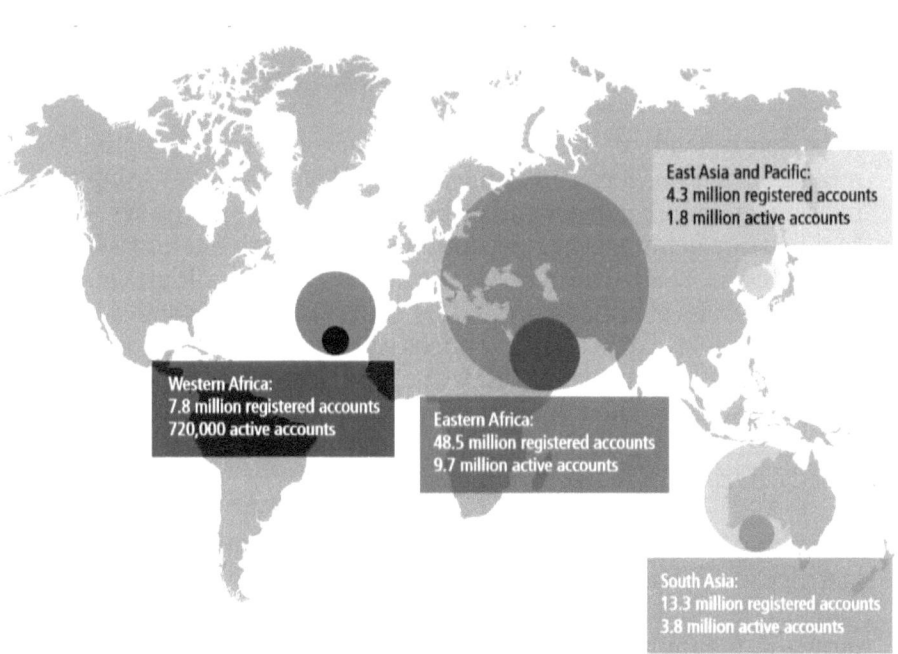

Source: GSMA - State of the Industry.

Figure 3.6 shows the number of registered and active mobile banking customer accounts by region, as mobile banking is a sub-sector of mobile telecommunication the graphic only shows a glimpse of the much larger mobile telecommunication sector in general. Nonetheless, the graphic correlates with results that found Somalia and neighbouring East African countries have the highest mobile uptake globally as well as the highest utilisation of mobile banking services in the world.

In early 2012, the Bill & Melinda Gates Foundation, the World Bank and the Gallop World Poll found that one-third of adults in Somalia had used mobile money. Furthermore, the 2012 MMU Global Mobile Money Adoption Survey revealed that Somalia had one of the world's highest rates of customer uptake. The World Bank's Global Financial Inclusion Database (Findex) recently revealed that Somalia was one of the most active mobile money markets: 26% of the population reported using mobiles to pay bills, which is the highest rate in the world, and 32% to send and receive money. Most of this mobile money activity has been driven by Telesom ZAAD. In early 2009 Telesom ZAAD succeeded in becoming the 5th telecommunication company in the world that provides MMT (mobile money transfer) technology to its customers, a remarkable achievement[43].

It is clearly evident that the Somali market is very receptive to mobile-based services and applications, as well as underlining the increasing Somali market and utilisation of mobile phone services. Mobile transactions occur predominantly through Sahal, EMAAL and Telesom Zaad. These service providers receive a high volume of transactions averaging around 34 transactions per customer on a regular weekly basis. These services were introduced in 2009 and now total 14 with Sahal, EMAAL and Telesom Zaad at the forefront[44]. Since their inception in 2009 limited innovation has taken place, and most of the mobile payment services are SMS-based catering for feature phones.

The global rise of mobile telecommunication utilisation during the last decade illustrates the impact of new technologies and the magnitude of changes that they have triggered. Unlike preceding network technologies, mobile phone networks can be set up quickly provided the spectrum agreements are in place. Thanks to competition, they also offer much improved services and lower

---

[43] World Bank/UNDP (2002) Somali Socio-Economic Survey 2011 (Washington DC, US: World Bank).

[44] Claire Pénicaud (2013), "State of the Industry: Results from the 2012 Global Mobile Money Adoption Survey," GSMA, London, UK.

prices both in terms of capabilities and in terms of information retrieval, overcoming typical problems of inefficiencies generated by monopolies in fixed networks[45].

Mobile networks provide the framework for the delivery of different services ranging from telephone calls and its variants (i.e. video phones, teleconferencing) to high-speed Internet access and very diverse services (SMS, mobile banking, video streaming, online games, tele-working, etc). This technology improves overall productivity by enhancing the capabilities of the labour force and the communication between firms. Users collaborate over long distances, exchange information wherever they travel, shop in global markets and carry useful data in their phones. The use of this infrastructure spreads to other industries and contributes to their profits thus affecting their overall growth. While the telecommunications industry is primarily affected by the infrastructure itself, the important spillovers of mobile networks repercuss in the other sectors of the economy[46].

Mobile Banking:

Mobile banking refers to financial services delivered via mobile networks and performed on a mobile phone, for example mobile transactions such as remittances and any other such payments delivered with the utilisation of mobile phones. As of 2012, Somalia has around 186 internet hosts. There were about 106,000 online users in the country in 2009. Moreover in the space of three years between 2008 and 2011 mobile subscribers doubled from 512,682 in 2008 to 1,089,540 in 2011 showing the rapid rise in mobile phone ownership.

Indeed, economists have noted the rise in mobile banking innovation in East Africa with the dominance of M-Pesa in Kenya and Zaad within Somalia. Zaad is a mobile banking service provided to major Somali telecommunication firms such as; Telesom and Hormuud Telecom and acts as the dominant money transfer system. Zaad has picked up more than 300,000 users

---

[45] Wellenius Bjorn (1993) "Telecommunications: World Bank experience and strategy" World Bank discussion papers, Washington, D.C.

[46] Gruber H, Koutroumpis P, 2011, Mobile telecommunications and the impact on economic development, Economic Policy, Vol: 67, Pages: 1-41

since its launch three years ago through the Telesom network. Payments and transactions are made which is incredibly efficient and secure enabling parents to send money to children at school or employers to pay their employees [47]. On average single customers are limited to transfers of $500 while accredited merchants can move up to $2,000. Most private sector businesses use the system and Telesom pays all of its employees using Zaad. Mobile Banking is increasingly becoming more popular with both regional Somali banks due to a wide array of factors, most notably the advantage of drastically cutting down the costs of providing service to the customers. For example an average teller or phone transaction costs about is $1 each, whereas an electronic transaction costs only about $0.10 each. Additionally, this new channel gives the bank the ability to advertise and up-sell their other banking products, which is a technique already adopted by Somali Mobile banking providers like Hormuud, Telesom, Golis and Somalia Telecom. For mobile banking to prosper; there already has to be a substantially large consumer base for mobile telecommunications which is the case within Somalia. Indeed, this can be seen by looking at the graph:

Fig 3.7: African Mobile Connection & Penetration Rate

Penetration Rate

No. Connections

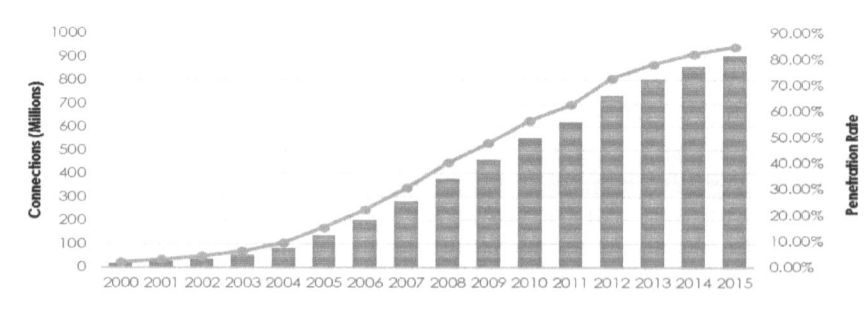

This graph displays the mobile connection and penetration rate on the African Continent and highlights the rapid rise in both mobile

---

[47] http://www.theglobeandmail.com/news/world/how-mobile-phones-are-making-cash-obsolete-in-africa/article12756675/

connections as well as penetration rates; with the later showing exponential growth from 2005 onwards. The forecasts suggest the trend will continue and indicates that mobile phones will become integral to the lives of Africans across the continent.

We've already seen companies like Starbucks adopt mobile payment, but it is assumed that in the next couple of years it will reach the tipping point of adoption where the majority of early adopters are using this technology. 617bn is forecast to be paid via mobile transactions with 418m users by 2016. Moreover, Africa and Asia will account for a staggering 60% of all such mobile payments.

In 2012, the Bill & Melinda Gates Foundation, the World Bank and the Gallup World Poll found that one-third of adults in Somalia had used mobile money. Furthermore, the 2012 MMU Global Mobile Money Adoption Survey revealed that Somalia had one of the world's highest rates of customer uptake. The World Bank's Global Financial Inclusion Database (Findex) recently revealed that Somalia was one of the most active mobile money markets: 26% of the population reported using mobiles to pay bills, which is the highest rate in the World, and 32% send and receive money.

Most of this mobile money activity has been driven by Telesom ZAAD. In early 2009, Telesom ZAAD succeeded in becoming the 5th global telecommunications company to provide MMT (mobile money transfer) technology to its customers - a remarkable achievement.

It is evident that the Somali market is very receptive to mobile-based services and applications, as well as underlining the increasing Somali market and utilisation of mobile phone services. Mobile transactions occur predominantly through Sahal, EMAAL and Telesom Zaad. These service providers receive a high volume of transactions averaging around 34 transactions per customer on a regular weekly basis. These services were introduced in 2009 and now total 14 - with Sahal, EMAAL and Telesom Zaad at the forefront. Since their inception in 2009, limited innovation has taken place, and most of the mobile payment services are SMS-based, catering for feature phones. According to some of the figures released by Samsung, 1 in 15 phones shipped are smartphones, this is predicted to increase to 1 in 5 or 6 in 2015. Given how integral mobile devices are in the Horn of Africa, services and products developed by banks in this region need to have a strong mobile strategy to cater for customer behaviours and usage patterns.

Figure 3.8: Mobile Subscribers in Somalia

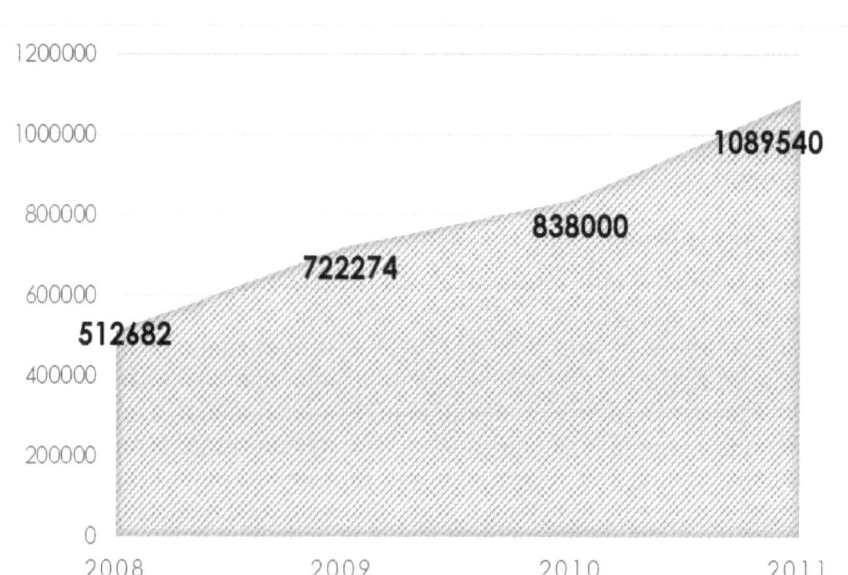

Mobile banking providers include: Hormuud Telecom, Golis Telecom, Somtel and the Somali Telecom Group (an umbrella for a number of companies). As well as providing mobile banking, the companies also provide Internet services and Wi-Fi technology. Mobile Banking can also be used by the service provider as a channel to advertise and up-sell their other products, which is a technique already adopted by Somali Mobile banking providers, like Telesom Zaad, Sahal and Emaal.

The procedure for mobile banking in Somalia is straightforward: the sender completes a form designed by the mobile banking provider stating how much he/she wants to send and to whom, once the money has been paid out to the designated recipient, the company sends a second confirmation text message to the sender of the cash confirming the transaction. Mobile operators sometimes send their subscribers texts with commercial advertising. Radio stations report high volumes of texts from listeners to inter-active programmes, as well as voice calls.

Somali mobile tariffs are among the cheapest in the world. International call rates are as low as 20 US cents per minute, helped by the fact that many networks channel international calls through the voice over Internet protocol (VOIP), rather than conventional phone lines[48].

The rapidly increasing number of Mobile Banking users can also be explained by the logic that it is a more secure way of banking in comparison to conventional means, due to the fact that it removes the necessity to carry cash. Another reason why mobile banking is becoming increasingly popular is that not only does it save the client time, but also provides the added convenience of allowing consumers to do their everyday banking, anytime, anywhere - as long as they are connected to the internet.

The trend looks set to continue, with analysts predicting year-on-year growth for mobile banking; they forecast a huge jump in terms of mobile phone payments to occur between 2012 and 2016.

4. Internet Services in Somalia

Internet usage in Africa has risen exponentially in recent times and is currently growing at a rapid rate. Africa has benefited immensely in recent years from the various technology infrastructure investments which have been made; they have lowered the wholesale prices for Internet bandwidth, due to affordable satellite access and the use of Fibre Optic links. Internet Broadband technology is becoming the preferred Internet access as opposed to Dial-Up and in many parts of Africa, Wi-Fi is prevalent, especially in hotels, airports, restaurants and public buildings. Somalia has likewise benefited from a rapid explosion in its Internet usage. There are various Internet providers in Somalia, and Global Internet Company is one which was founded in 2003 by a consortium of Somalia's leading telecom companies including Hormuud and NationLink. It provides various services such as: dial-up, DSL and some point-to-point wireless access. However, since the early 2000's, an array of telecommunication companies in Somalia - including major players such as: Global Internet, Golis Telecom, Telesom and Somtel – have succeeded in

---

[48] Nenova, T. and Harford, T. (2004) 'Anarchy and Invention: How Does Somalia's Private Sector Cope Without Government?' Public Policy for the Private Sector, No.280 (Washington DC, US: World Bank).

providing consumers with internet services throughout the country, through a variety of microwave, satellite and fibre optics networks.

Despite these commendable achievements in terms of Internet provision and usage; there are continuing bottlenecks that have prevented the Internet sector from reaching its full potential. Indeed, if Somalia's mobile telecommunications sector is innovative and cheap, then Somalia's Internet communications sector has been expensive and slow. The reason for this is the continuing use of Dial-Up, as opposed to newer forms of Internet provision. Although Dial-Up is the most subscribed to service, by consumers within Somalia; this is simply due to the fact that it is the cheapest option, at around $30 (£18) a month per computer. It is however painfully slow - less than 56kbs.

Wi-Fi internet provision, however, has been expanded throughout various key public buildings, airports and universities – across major urban centres in Mogadishu, Puntland and Somaliland.

Fibre Optic Cable developments: Importantly, there have been major developments with regards to Somalia's internet communications sector and perhaps the biggest development has been the roll out of Fibre Optic cables. Although the Fibre Optic cable option has been mooted for a while; it has only recently gained traction and been implemented in Mogadishu and Somaliland, in particular.

The advantages of optical fibres dwarf those of conventional Dial-Up and other cumbersome Internet services. For example, several miles of optical cable can be made cheaper than equivalent lengths of copper wire, which are used in traditional Internet communications in Africa. Also, they possess a higher carrying capacity and a more reliable signal, which is crucial for enhanced Internet communications development. The loss of signal in optical fibre is less than in copper wire. Optical fibres are ideally suited for carrying digital information, which is especially useful in computer networks. Another major advantage, which can be applied to the case of Somalia, is the fact that Fibre Optic cables are far safer - unlike the various copper cables littering urban centres. This is the case because no electricity is passed through optical fibres, hence limiting any fire hazard.

In terms of infrastructure and installation, Optical Fibre cables weigh much less than a comparable copper wire cable. Optical fibres can be drawn to smaller diameters than copper wire. Fibre optic cables take up less space in the ground.

CASE STUDY: EASSy Fibre Optic cable

WIOCC, together with local shareholder Dalkom Somalia, have announced the launch of connectivity to and from Somalia. The service will offer a direct link between Mogadishu and the rest of the world, with capacity availability ranging between 2Mbps to 10Gbps and above. Hortel's fibre network will provide Liquid Telecom's customers – fixed and mobile operators, wholesale carriers and enterprises – with reliable, robust and fast connectivity in Southern and central Somalia. Somalia has until now been served exclusively by satellite - with high cost and limited bandwidth. WIOCC and Dalkom, will be the first commercial operation with international fibre optic directly into Mogadishu. Fibre network, will reduce the cost of international bandwidth and drive significant performance improvement. Mohamed Ahmed Jama, CEO of Dalkom Somalia, added, *"As we have seen in other African countries over recent years, access to affordable, high-speed, international connectivity has a significant impact on economic, political and social development and improvements. To complement the new connectivity to EASSy, Dalkom Somalia is building a fibre optic metropolitan area network that will extend connectivity to customers within Mogadishu and the rest of Somalia."*

CASE STUDY: SomCable Fibre Optic Cable

Image 1: SomCable workers placing the Fibre Optic

SomCable has emerged in recent years as a major force in Somaliland's telecommunications sector and has succeeded in providing fierce competition to Telesom and Somtel. SomCable has origins in Djibouti and the Middle East and its phenomenal rise in recent years has been due to its sustained focus on innovation and investment. The entire region of Somaliland was given access to next-generation broadband in 2012, thanks to a £35m rollout of a Fibre Optics cable passing through Djibouti and the Red Sea; work carried out by Somcable along with other investors. The East African submarine Fibre optic cable EASSy, runs along the seabed along the coast of East Africa from Sudan to South Africa. A direct connection to it, opens the way for faster and cheaper internet services in Somaliland. In April 2011, Djibouti became the latest country to hook up to the EASSy cable.

The investment will see 1200 Km of new fibre being laid to bring speeds of up to 100Mbit/s to homes and businesses in the region.

The Chief Executive of Somcable, Mike Cothill, said that the rollout would stand as a "...*flagship example of what can be achieved with new technology in the emerging market... we expect to cover 80 to 90 per cent of the county with fibre-to-the-*

rural or fibre-to-the-towns by 2013, with the rest of the county being connected either through wireless technologies. We think demand will be high, especially from businesses, and we hope to have our first customers up and running on the new services by end of the year."[49]

5. Economic Benefits of Improved Telecommunications

A responsive and vibrant telecommunications sector is a vital proponent of socio-economic development as it fosters business activity and increased consumer transactions. Along with financial institutions, it acts as an interface between business networks and the foundation for their structures. Whether ordering a product or buying spare parts, transferring money or finalising a transaction, telecommunications services are essential, especially in Somalia which already has the historical distinction of being an oral nation. The most important aspect of the telecommunications sector is that it has a substantial multiplier effect on the rest of the economy whereby other sectors such as: finance, public sector, education etc. are buoyed by the telecommunications sector. Media is among the many sectors that rely on the telecommunications infrastructure. Local radio stations in Mogadishu and across Somalia have correspondents who use mobile telephones to broadcast the news from all over Somalia[50].

The telecommunications sector, along with the remittances sector in Somalia, tends to be the highest employer, especially of university graduates. One such reason is that university graduates tend to be young (usually under 30) and as a result they are Internet savvy and well acquainted with mobile phones, compared to the older generation in Somalia. Also, because most of these telecommunication firms have a commitment to innovation, it is only logical that they recruit from university graduates who are usually woefully overlooked in Somalia. In addition, improved telecommunications services enables business and employees of the public sector to increase their productivity and efficiency, which also has a knock-on, positive effect for the general economy. There are also major challenges faced by the telecommunications

---

[49] http://www.realwire.com/releases/Somcable-selects-Bluwan-to-roll-out-next-generation-broadband-across-the-Horn-of-Africa

[50] Yusuf, A. (2006). Somali Enterprises: Making Peace their Business. *International Alert*. P474 – 508. London, UK

sector which need to be addressed. In particular, Somalia has a crumbling telecommunications infrastructure with telephone wires and pylons scattering urban cities to the extent that it becomes a safety hazard.

Investors interested in Somalia's telecommunications sector will be advised that there are no barriers to entry, which enables foreign firms to invest and develop significantly. As a result, there are many lucrative opportunities for foreign firms to invest. In particular, the absence of a monopolistic, state-owned telecommunications firm, only serves to highlight the opportunity that these firms face, as most foreign firms suffer from discriminate practices adopted by some developing states. Furthermore, in Somalia there exists the absence of a rigorous, regulatory environment and as a result; foreign firms do not have to worry about the issue of taxes, bureaucracy and unnecessary red tape - which is often a major impediment to investment in many other African states.

Telecommunication infrastructure already exists in Somalia in the form of telecommunication towers and equipment installed by these private sector, major firms. Foreign investors need not worry about such issues. However, with their expertise and capital, foreign firms have the advantage of entering and operating within an already large and ever-expanding lucrative market. For example, a study by the Broadcasting Board of Governors - the parent company of Voice of America -shows that Somalia has the highest personal ownership of mobile phones after Nigeria. BBG claims South Central Somalia has the higher rates of SMS (text) usage, television, newspapers, mobile apps, and Internet than in other regions. These facts alone show that the market for mobile users in Somalia is huge and will only grow larger, due to the potential demographic explosion that Somalia may benefit from in the future as 70% of Somalia's population is under 30 with over half under 20.

In regards to Somalia's Internet communications sector; further investment and development in such a key sector will help to stimulate greater economic activity.

Throughout various countries and cities, research has consistently shown a robust correlation between high levels of Internet usage and economic growth and development. Increased Internet provision throughout Somalia will have a major Multiplier Effect; which will touch all parts of the economy.

Increased efficiency in Internet services will enable SMEs throughout Somalia to prosper and develop their business in a more efficient and transformative way. Therefore, it is no surprise that many Somali businesses and the Somali private sector at large have all greeted the news of incoming Fibre Optic cable technologies and Wi-Fi internet provision with excitement.

Such crucial developments will no doubt assist Somalia in its economic growth and the modernisation of its economy.

6. Summary

Somalia is in the midst of a telecommunications boom, driven by private investors who have created a mass market with the cheapest calling rates in Africa.

Private investors have put more than $194m into Somalia's telecommunications sector over the last ten years. However, for Somalia to truly benefit from such a vibrant telecommunications sector, it is crucial that it encourages and tries to attract more Foreign Direct Investment (FDI).

There is still much scope for improvement in infrastructure and investment in Somalia's telecommunications sector, which is evident by the fact that many international NGOs and private companies, such as big hotels, have their own VSAT systems for reliable Internet access and direct telephone access to the rest of the world.

CASE STUDY: Huawei investment in Africa's telecommunications sector:

Huawei, whose name can be translated from Chinese as 'China Can', is the largest telecom equipment manufacturer and network solutions provider in China and the third-largest in the world. It has adopted an FDI policy of expanding aggressively in Africa in the past decade. Such has been the success of Huewi, that its operations and investment ventures in Africa account for about 12 to 13 per cent of Huawei's revenue (about US$ 3.5 billion from Africa, 2010).

In less than a decade, Huawei has penetrated almost every market around the world, investing heavily in its business and technology product lines, which include: fixed networks, mobile networks, data communications, optical networks, software and services, and terminals.[51]

---

[51] http://knowledge.wharton.upenn.edu/article/huawei-technologies-a-chinese-trail-blazer-in-africa/

CHAPTER FOUR
THE ENERGY SECTOR

Introduction:

Oil and gas exploration is indeed important in a country's economic development as it enables a trade-off between a state's natural resources and investment and increased GDP. It is no surprise to find that some of the fastest growing economies in Africa belong to oil producing states such as: Nigeria and Mozambique. In recent years, East Africa has emerged as the new frontier for the global race for oil and gas exploration and contracts. Recent oil and gas discoveries in East Africa have included various states such as Kenya and South Sudan, a swell as other African states which have all succeeded in finding a substantial deposit of gas reserves. Somalia is no exception and in the past few years, oil and gas exploration activities have accelerated throughout Somalia and, in particular, the regions of Puntland and Somaliland.

According to development economists, oil and gas production can act as an economic blessing to a state, as well as a "Resource Curse", whereby there is increased dependency on natural resources and increased instability, due to intense competition over natural resources. It is this objective look at the economic opportunities in Somalia presented by oil and gas exploration, that has led to us formulating this report.

In order to collate this chapter, we conducted in-depth economic research on the oil and gas exploration potential existing within Somalia and the oil and gas exploration contracts dispensed to foreign majors and oil companies in recent years.

In the past couple of years, Somalia has experienced an economic and political renaissance, which has encouraged sustained investment in various sectors; most notably within its oil and gas sector. Indeed, the existence of natural resources and particularly oil and gas may act as a crucial foundation of economic development; it enables increased job creation and linkages within the economy.

I believe wholeheartedly that a focused strategy on promoting the oil and gas exploration potential of the state will play a crucial role in fostering economic growth and creating jobs. This chapter helps to publicise these major trends in Somalia's oil and gas exploration to a wider, global audience, which we feel - in an era of globalization - can only be positive.

1. BACKGROUND OF THE OIL & GAS SECTOR IN SOMALIA

The Federal Republic of Somalia was firmly established following the transitional period in September 2012 and the emergence of a new government led by President Hassan Sheikh. However, despite these political changes, Somalia is still plagued by prior issues and notable amongst them is the issue of energy production.

Many citizens lack basic electricity or energy options. In economic terms, the availability and utilisation of energy is crucial to a healthy, robust economy and currently Somalia is lagging behind other African states in terms of energy options. However, despite this, Somalia has a genuinely favourable geography and climate which is conducive to energy production and particularly alternative energy sources. Also, despite 20 years of warfare, the various electricity firms have managed to provide urban centres of Somalia with sustained electricity, which does not fall prey to constant power cuts as is the norm in many other richer African nations such as, Nigeria. In addition, the Somali populace has proven to be truly innovative in terms of meeting household energy needs.

Up to 90% of the Somali population has no access to electricity. Although it does serious damage to the country's environment, 87% of Somalia's energy consumption comes from traditional biomass-type fuels: charcoal or firewood. Imported petroleum products account for 11%, while electric power generation, using diesel fuel accounts for 2%.

Two-thirds of the Somali population live in rural areas, with a significant nomadic population reflecting a geographical 'scatter' of energy needs. This fact, combined with the destruction of the nation's energy infrastructure during the civil war, explains the basic nature of the energy sector in Somalia.

When examining the energy infrastructure in Somalia, it is clear to see that the main sources of energy are imported petroleum and local biomass resources. Petroleum is imported in the form of refined diesel, petrol, and aviation gas, all of which are used for transportation and electric power generation. Other imported petroleum products including kerosene and natural gas, which are used for cooking by certain segments of the urban community. Kerosene, in addition to cooking, is also used for illumination in the form of kerosene lamps by a large number of consumers.

These Independent Power Producers (IPPs) generally have a monopoly on energy generation and electricity in Somalia, yet they suffer from heavy operational and maintenance costs of diesel generators. It is no surprise therefore that the electricity tariff rate in Somalia is amongst the highest in Africa at approximately $1.00- 1.40 /kWh5. This issue needs to be addressed immediately, because as global consumption, fuel costs and unstable imported fuel supply problems continue to rise, electricity costs will also rise. These high costs to firms are already restricting business development and, as it increases, it will be too expensive for the majority of business and ordinary consumers in Somalia. For power producers, it is becoming difficult to be financially viable and still be sustainable in the long-term. As a result, the Government should begin to draft a plan whereby they prioritise energy investment from private and public sources. The government of Somalia should then focus on attracting much needed major investment, which will enable them to upgrade, diversify and modernise this important sector.

Electricity in Somalia:

In 1991 when the Siad Barre regime collapsed and the last vestiges of central government were overthrown, the electricity infrastructure, including wires, poles and generators were taken over by regional authorities, business tycoons and various factions. This meant that although electricity was available, there was no unified power grid - leading to the emergence of independent providers and an ad hoc system, whereby neighbours pay neighbours for electricity which has since continued unabated. It is for this reason and other factors that Somalis continue to face some of the highest electricity prices in the world.

Somali consumers currently pay $0.80 to $1.30/kWh for electricity which is extremely high, even by African standards - Ethiopians pay of $0.20/kWh.

The situation is so dire that private generator owners charge neighbours increasingly excessive prices, depending on their electricity usage. Diesel generators have been imported by the various middle-class Somali families and usually these generators are from the Middle East. This is troublesome as it leads to an unhealthy dependence on Middle Eastern importers and the erratic price of diesel. Currently private enterprises provide localized electricity in certain urban centres for those that can afford it. The supply is fragmented and there is no regulatory framework.

Primary energy needs in Somalia are small (with average requirements of 20–50 Watt-hours per person per day) - for cooking, lighting in the home, supporting the uplifting of water from bore-holes (for personal use, watering livestock or plants), as well as for street lighting. Somalia's dynamic private sector also requires energy to underpin and enable their businesses to grow and expand.

Biomass Energy:

Biomass energy refers to a wide range of natural organic fuels such as wood, charcoal, agricultural residues and animal waste, often used in its traditional and unprocessed form. The overwhelming majority of Somalia; (around 90%) relies on biomass energy in its main forms such as wood fire or charcoal which resulted in wide scale deforestation within Somalia and destruction of the environment. Throughout Somalia, charcoal is the primary form of non-biomass fuel and it is used in a variety of different ways, namely cooking and illuminating households through archaic fossil-fuelled wicker and oil lamps, with kerosene being the most common fuel.

It seems scarcely believable to Westerners that oil lamps and kerosene are still being used in the world and even more shockingly that they provide for the majority of household energy needs in Somalia.

Charcoal production at a sub-industrial level is one of the primary causes of deforestation in the developing world and this is especially the case in Somalia, where the destruction of such a large quantity of trees has resulted in desertification; adversely impacting on the environment. In addition, health side effects of charcoal include the increased occurrences of respiratory illnesses. The lack of a strong, central government is what paved the way for the illegal charcoal trade to flourish. As a result, the charcoal business has become a source of livelihood for many families displaced in the civil unrest. The charcoal is produced in remote, rural areas and then brought to urban centres for use and export. For many poor Somali households in such rural areas, the illicit charcoal has acted as the only source of income, due to the expensive electricity costs and a lack of other energy alternatives. The illegal charcoal is then mostly shipped for export to markets in the Middle East, according to the UN Monitoring Report. Currently 80% of Somalia's charcoal output is exported mainly to Saudi Arabia, Yemen and United Arab Emirates (UAE). The charcoal produced in Somalia is mainly produced in South and Central Somalia's riverside areas of Shabelle and Juba.

The charcoal export ban came into effect in Somalia under the previous TFG administration with the UN Security Council passing a stern resolution and Obama's Executive Order. Alternatively, it is incumbent upon the central government to explore other sources of energy such as development of oil and gas projects, which can eliminate poverty in Somalia and replace the use of biomass. The main reason the TFG requested its ban at the time and the UN and the US (under an Executive Order from President Obama) acquiesced, is because the illicit charcoal trade acted as an income generating enterprise for the Al-Shabaab terrorist organisation. At the time Al-Shabaab were benefiting substantially from the illegal charcoal trade, as they had at that time full control of the major Southern port city of Kismaayo. On the 25th February 2012, the UN Security Council banned the export of charcoal from Somalia. In addition, the Executive Order issued by US President Obama came into effect on the 20th July 2012, banning charcoal exportation from Somalia.

In recent years, East Africa has emerged as the new frontier for the global race in oil and gas discoveries. Recent oil and gas discoveries in East Africa have included various states such as: Kenya and South Sudan, notably other African states have found substantial deposits of gas reserves and in particular, Mozambique. Nevertheless, East Africa states such as Tanzania and Uganda are ensuring that this region remains relevant and crucial as a potential oil and gas region.

Somalia is judged to possess significant, untapped and underexplored natural resources in the region of 100 billion barrels of oil.

Furthermore, there is also likely to be vast natural gas reserves in Somali waters (Indian Ocean), particularly in the Somali Basin. Indeed, the real problem of future oil and gas supplies is not the potential physical availability of resources, but the accessibility of such potential resources which is even more precarious in a post-conflict state such as Somalia.

According to the Eastern African petroleum experts, there are 12 sedimentary basins in Somalia, which have barely been explored with only 63 wells drilled in the whole of Somalia. If you compare this to the North Sea, which has drilled around 4230 wells, it is clear that this is a sixth of the size of Somalia's sedimentary basins. Some of Somali basins include: Mandera-Luq Basin, Bur Hakaba Uplift, costal basins from Adale to Ras-Kamboni, the Somali embayment which occupies from Nugal to central regions, Nugal uplifts, and the northern coast Guban and Dharoor valleys.

Hence, around the Somali embayment and Nugal uplift is believed to be the most promising regions in the onshore oil and gas development, while the Indian Ocean Somali Basin is the most offshore prospect (APPG, 1976).

Somalia has emerged from two decades of civil strife to stability and this has enticed various petroleum companies to take a gamble on Somalia's considerable potential reserves.

The Puntland region of Somalia was technically the first part of Somalia to engage in oil and gas drilling in January 2012 when it signed a deal with Range Resources and Africa Oil.

If one is to examine Somalia's oil and gas potential, it is incumbent to delve into history as Somalia has long been touted as having untapped reserves of natural resources. When aligned to the fact that the Somali peninsula is so close in proximity to the oil rich Gulf Arab states such as Saudi Arabia and Yemen, it increases the likelihood of Somalia containing such deposits.

About 60 years ago, during the early 1950's, Agip and Sinclair Oil Corporation began to study the petroleum geology of Somalia which proved favourable at the time. Subsequently, companies have flocked to Somalia whenever possible. Sinclair Oil Corporation drilled more than 50 wells in the south (some for stratigraphic and some for oil production purposes) and worked from the mid-Fifties to mid-Sixties without commercial oil discovery.

Eni (previously known as Agip) worked from the Fifties to the Eighties and abandoned Block 31 (Puntland) in force majeure, following the collapse of the central government in 1991.

In 1991 - prior to the fall of the central government - a report of Northeast Africa by the World Bank and U.N. - ranked Somalia second only to Sudan as the top prospective producer, especially considering the fact that it lies in a regional oil window across the Gulf of Aden.

Another optimistic seismic analysis report proposed that there may be monumental oil deposits in this region, similar to those of the North Sea or Kuwaiti oil reserves. Somalia is one of the last frontiers for oil and gas in eastern Africa. Prior to the fall of his beleaguered administration, the late President of Somalia, Siad Barre, succeeded in negotiating contracts with oil majors including: Royal Dutch Shell, Concoo, BP and Chevron.

These agreements were in the form of contracts and by the time the majors were ready to drill, anarchy had descended onto the Somali capital and forced Siad Barre from power. Nevertheless, when examining these oil contracts with the majors it is important to note that the contracts were declared "force majeure" and the oil majors have been biding their time ever since, waiting for a stable government in Somalia to negotiate with.

With the election of the current President in September 2012, the increased international recognition and presence of Somalia, these oil majors have advocated for their oil contracts to be honoured. In response to this scenario, the current Federal Government of Somalia has called for the return and prioritisation of these oil majors, in order to renegotiate their oil contracts. Abdullahi Haider, a senior adviser to Somalia's Ministry of Energy, has also stated to international media outlets that it is the Federal

Government's position that these oil majors contracts be given due precedence.[52]

2. ALTERNATIVE FORMS OF ENERGY IN SOMALIA

Wind Energy:

Around two-thirds of the African population are without electricity and this situation is worse for Somalis, with up to 90% lacking any electricity. Due to these distressing facts, it is imperative that there is sustained investment in alternative and renewable energy resources such as windmills and wind turbines, which will go some way to addressing this electricity shortage, whilst also being more environmentally friendly.

The Somali climate is often windy, especially in mountainous areas such as Sanaag region in North Somalia and as such introducing windmill and wind turbine technology would be a practical and sustainable idea. The majority of inhabitants in Somalia are overwhelmingly rural and they can benefit from alternative, renewable energy sources: wind, solar, and hydro energy - which many other emerging African economies are benefiting from. The advantages of these alternative energy sources far outweigh the negatives and they are much more environmentally friendly.

Some optimistic analysts have claimed that wind energy may potentially replace or decrease the use of petroleum for various uses across the country. Moreover, this form of energy generation reduces the adverse impact on the already besieged environment and the precious hard currency of the country. Another reason why Somalia should actively pursue wind energy is because it is plentiful, readily available, and capturing its power does not deplete natural resources.

The available information about wind energy, shows that 50% of the Somali peninsula has wind speeds suitable for electric energy production (in this instance; wind speeds higher than 6 meters per second), at a cost competitive rate with the energy generated from diesel power plants.

In 70% of the territory, the wind energy is competitive with small conventional thermal plants for water pumping or for rural

---

[52] http://www.reuters.com/article/2012/10/02/somalia-oil-exploration-idUSL6E8L2O7D20121002

electrification (wind speeds greater than 5 meters per second). In 95% of the Somali territory, diesel-powered water pumps can be profitably replaced by windmills. In addition, windmills are a very scalable investment, particularly when wind pattern maps are developed. They are functional enough to offer multiple purposes such as grinding corn, millet, and wheat.

The mechanical energy generated by windmills is not only used to power necessary machinery, such as for grinding grain, but they can also be the right energy source for borehole pumps in rural areas.

Wind Turbines:

Another form of alternative energy linked to the windmill methods are wind turbines, which are used to convert kinetic energy from the wind into mechanical energy in a process known as wind power. In so far as the mechanical energy is used to produce electricity, then the device may be called a wind turbine or wind power plant. Today's wind turbines are manufactured in a wide range of vertical and horizontal axis types. The large grid-connected arrays of turbines are becoming an increasingly important source of wind power-produced commercial electricity and their introduction in Somalia could help to power homes for millions of Somalis and public facilities across the country.

The introduction of wind turbines is expected to provide up to 30 KW of continuous power to 20-30 houses. They can be assembled within a week by trained technicians and more importantly they will go a long way to alleviating the reliance on expensive electric generation.

Wind turbine energy is a cheaper option to the diesel generators which currently provide nearly 100% of the energy that Somalia uses. Diesel generators are very expensive to operate because all diesels are imported from the Gulf. The turbine is scalable and can be used by hospitals, schools, and other businesses that want reliable energy. Somali's energy needs are small: 20–50 kWh/per day per person for cooking, lighting in homes and streets. Despite this, the method of using diesel generators turns it into an expensive process.

In 2012, utility scale wind turbines ranged from about $1.3 million to $2.2 million per MW (installed). Smaller farm or residential scale turbines cost less overall, but are more expensive per kilowatt of energy producing capacity. Wind turbines under 100 kilowatts cost roughly $3,000 to $8,000 per kilowatt of capacity. A 10 KW machine (the size needed to power a large building) might have an installed cost of $50,000-$80,000 (or more) depending on the tower type, height, and the cost of installation. The overall cost of building and equipping both windmills and wind turbines is affordable to businesses and rural communities, especially if they pool their resources, though ideally the funds and know-how of foreign investors would prove advantageous. In particular, it may prove to be more beneficial if there are increased Public Private Partnerships (PPP's) to overcome these expensive installation and maintenance costs.

Without power, Somalia will face serious challenges in expanding its economy. Energy access and "energy poverty" remain significant concerns for all of Somalia. The Federal Somali Government must develop National Renewable Energy Action Plans (NREAPs) detailing sectorial and technology-specific targets and policy measures. It is highly feasible for public and private partnerships to invest in large wind farms, providing the country with much needed cheap, clean and sustainable energy.

Case Study: Wind Turbines at Hargeisa (Egal) International Airport:

With the support of USAID, the Somaliland administration installed the first wind farm in the region in 2013, which will power the Egal International Airport in Hargeisa. The five 20kW turbines will be managed under a public private partnership (PPP) structure, and will showcase the potential of wind power for investors; while being used as a place for power companies, Ministry engineers, and electrical engineering students to learn more about renewable energy.[53]

Solar Power:

Somalia's climatic environment, with over 3,000 hours of high and constant sunlight annually, is conducive to solar power as the sun

---
[53] http://somalilandinvest.net/case-studies/energy-case-studies/somaliland-installs-first-pilot-wind-farm

can then be used to power the urban centres in Somalia. Solar power can then be channelled into many small or medium sized aero generators; photovoltaic solar systems to contribute to decentralized rural and urban energy systems.

Given the small energy requirements for households, solar-powered lamps and cookers for domestic use would be extremely applicable and, within Mogadishu, solar-powered streetlights have succeeded in improving safety in the neighbourhoods they were placed near.

Solar cookers of various types have been developed – as have more efficient biomass cook stoves (requiring less firewood). Greater production, distribution and use of such cookers would greatly help the environment as well as improving the health of women and children (less risk of respiratory diseases) and ameliorating the lives and security of women who would no longer need to walk such long distances.

Solar power is currently used throughout Somalia at the basic level in rural areas and remote healthcare centres. However, it would prove to be far more beneficial if the government of Somalia utilised solar power to provide energy for its public offices and schools, etc.

Tidal power and hydroelectric power:

Somalia has the unique advantage of having the longest coastline in Africa and being situated strategically at the mouth of the Red Sea in the North and facing the Indian Ocean in the central and Southern regions. As a result, Somalia could in theory benefit from tidal energy which is a form of hydropower that converts the energy of tides into useful forms of power - mainly electricity. This is particularly crucial and interesting because tidal power has potential for future electricity generation. Tides are more predictable than wind energy and solar power.

However, expectations need to be tempered based on the fact that few countries, including advanced economies, have benefited from tidal power. Indeed, it is no surprise to find that amongst alternative sources of renewable energy, tidal power has traditionally suffered from relatively high costs and limited availability of sites with sufficiently high tidal ranges or flow velocities, thus constricting its total availability.

Hydroelectric power provides an interesting form of alternative energy. Flowing water creates energy that can be captured and turned into electricity, this in essence is hydroelectric power or hydropower.

Before touching on the advantages of hydroelectric energy, it is crucial for us to understand the dynamics of this alternative form of energy. To harness energy from flowing water, the water must be controlled through the creation of a large reservoir or dam. Water is then channelled through tunnels within the dam and this energy of water flowing through the dam's tunnels causes the turbines to turn. The turbines make generators move which in turn produce large amounts of electricity.

Experienced technical engineers are required in order to control the amount of water being sent through the dam. The process used to control this flow of water is called the intake system whereby a lot of energy is needed. Most of the tunnels to the turbines are open, and millions of gallons of water flow through them. When less energy is needed, engineers slow down the intake system by closing some of tunnels.

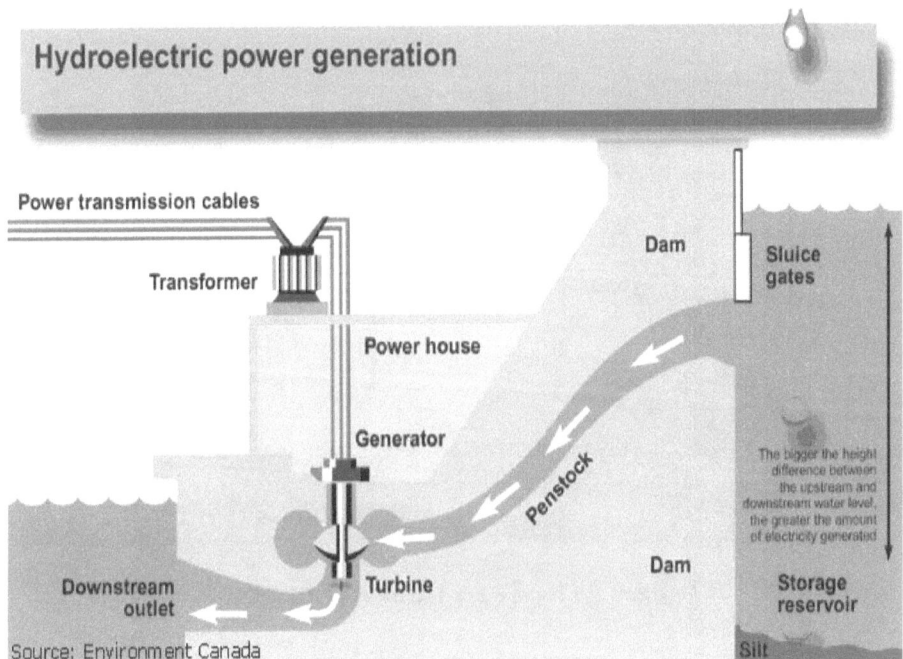

Image 2 : Graphic representation of the dynamics of hydroelectric power

The advantages of utilising hydroelectric power for energy needs in Somalia are plentiful. Firstly, Somalia, and in particular the Southern regions, contain prominent, powerful rivers such as the Juba and the Shabelle rivers. Somalia, although not as blessed as its neighbour Ethiopia with the potential of the legendary River Nile, can still benefit substantially through the adoption of hydroelectric power through its own main rivers.

A major environmental benefit of hydroelectric power is that Hydroelectricity relies on water, which is a clean, renewable energy source and Somalia during rainy seasons can benefit from this. In addition, the use of hydroelectric power has been used throughout developing and developed economies to provide their populace with the necessary energy needs. On average, states that utilise hydroelectric power effectively succeed in using such means to meet 90% of their energy needs. Western examples include the Hoover Dam and the Inga dam in the Congo - with such huge hydroelectric potential that it could light up much of Africa.

Image 3 The Inga Dam in Congo

When applied directly to Somalia's energy needs, it is clear that hydroelectric power has substantial potential to meet the energy needs of the 10 million citizens within Somalia. However, for this to become a genuine reality, it is crucial that the Federal Government of Somalia seek to attract foreign direct investment (FDI) or Public Private Partnerships in the alternative energy sector, whereby such monumental hydroelectric plants can be established. Indeed, the Ethiopian government has a history of significant infrastructure spending, yet the Ethiopian government has been seeking investors for their Great Dam project on the River Nile.

In addition, to benefit from hydroelectric power, the necessary expertise and technical knowledge is required as engineers will be tasked with the overseeing and implementation of hydroelectric power. Therefore, the government of Somalia could choose to bring in foreign experts or to utilise their educated diaspora members from abroad who have practised or studied engineering.

3. ENERGY SECTOR REGULATIONS

Regulations outlining the powers and limits of energy firms are often highly complex and require a high level of development to implement. With Somalia undergoing a gradual shift into a post-conflict state, it is crucial that the Federal Government of Somalia enacts legislation which will provide the energy sector with the necessary regulatory environment.

Currently, Somalia has passed a Draft Energy Law which it hopes will provide the energy sector with a framework to operate within. Regional administrations such as Somaliland and Puntland succeeded in passing an Energy Law, although they remain rudimentary in nature. Currently, there is a lack of a genuine regulatory environment in terms of energy policies. However, with the recent international donor conferences based on Somalia, there has been a concerted effort to assist the nascent Somali central government to create energy regulatory bodies and institutions. For example, at the Istanbul Conference of 2010 the suitability of alternative energy for Somalia was discussed. More importantly, the recent Brussels Compact deal for post-conflict states - which was adopted by Somalia - has provided significant funding for Somalia's energy needs and particularly its alternative energy needs.

4. OIL & GAS EXPLORATION IN SOMALIA

When touching on oil and gas exploration in Somalia it is crucial to mention the position advanced by regional administrations such as Puntland and Somaliland - as they have been the most active in terms of granting exploration rights to foreign oil companies, prior to the creation of the Federal Government of Somalia in September 2012.

Puntland:

The Puntland state of Somalia was formed in 1998 and forms a key foundational stone in the federal structure of Somalia. Incidentally, Puntland also sits on perhaps the most promising block - the Nugaal block which researchers have claimed may have the most potential in terms of oil resources in Somalia and possibly East Africa as a whole.

Puntland began negotiations with various foreign oil firms to explore its own oil and gas prospects in the mid-2000s. According to its own estimates, there could be reserves of up to 4 billion barrels, worth about $500 billion at today's prices, in its two drilling blocks alone. If the other future oil and gas prospects reserves across Somalia reach 100 billion of barrels, then this could all potentially be worth circa $12,500 billion at today's oil prices.

The Puntland administration in October 2005 granted Range Resources a majority stake in two sizable land-based mineral and hydrocarbon exploration licenses, in addition to offshore rights. The onshore Nugaal and Dharoor Valley blocks in question span over 14,424 km2 and 24,908 km2, respectively. Two years later, Range Resources obtained a 100% interest in the two blocks and concurrently farmed out 80% of that share to Canmex Minerals (which later became Africa Oil).

In January 2007, Puntland signed the Puntland Product Sharing Agreement (PSA) a royalty based and profit sharing agreement with Range Resources Limited and Africa oil. However, in 2009 with the accession of new President of Puntland Abdirahman Mohamud Farole, Puntland succeeded in renegotiating the profit sharing agreement with Range Resources to ensure more favourable terms for the region.

Following on from this, in 2012, the Puntland government gave the green light to the first official oil exploration project in Puntland and Somalia at large - which was led by the Canadian oil company Africa Oil (the former Canmex Minerals) and its partner Range Resources, which began in earnest initial drilling in the Shabeel-1 well on Puntland's Dharoor Block in March 2012.

In addition to drilling two wells, Range Resources built an airstrip and deployed 250 troops, led by South African security contractors, to counter Al-Shabaab.

Image 4 Puntland Dharoor oil field.

In addition, Range Resources and Africa Oil were not able to begin exploration in the potentially lucrative Nugaal block because the Somaliland administration sent its forces to expand into territory which they believed belonged to them, which also happened to encroach on the Western Nugaal block. Indeed, this issue has caused much tension between both sides as both Somaliland and Puntland have claimed the Nugaal block as their own and given out contracts overlapping this block. In particular, this scenario has shown the possible negative ramifications of oil exploration in Somalia which I will touch on in detail later on in the report.

Somaliland:

Somaliland is a self-declared state in Somalia, which is situated in the North-West of Somalia - generally recognised as an autonomous region in Somalia. Due to its location at the mouth of the Red Sea and its close proximity to Yemen (which is predicted to hold over 1 billion barrels of oil) the Somaliland region has been touted as a potentially oil prospective region in Somalia. It is for this reason and due to its relative stability in the past 22 years, that

Somaliland has been the most active in trying to entice investors and grant contracts for oil exploration rights to foreign firms. Indeed Somaliland has claimed that it may begin oil exploration as early as 2014, according to its natural resources minister Hussein Abdi Dualeh.[54]

A roll call of oil companies which have signed exploration and production sharing agreements with the Somaliland administration includes: Australian-based Jacka Resources, Petrosoma, London-listed Ophir Energy, DNO and Genel Energy, which is headed by former BP chief executive Tony Hayward, which all aim to start extensive exploration activities soon. Genel signed an exploration and potential product sharing agreement with the Somaliland administration. Indeed, this entrant in the Somali oil scene was considerable as it is the largest oil firm in Turkey. It is has already began surveying and aims to begin drilling in mid-2015. It also possesses a £2 billion market cap and is funding 100% of the exploration program in the Odewayne block until May 2015. Genel has about $1bln allocated for its operations in Somaliland and has even allocated around $40million just for the surveys.

Jacka Resources was the first firm to make a foray into the oil sector in Somaliland in April 2012 when it announced that it entered into an agreement with Petrosoma Limited to become Operator and a 50% equity holder in Blocks 6,7 (partial) and 10 (partial) - located onshore Somaliland, which are the subject of a Production Sharing Agreement ("PSA") with the Government of Somaliland. The PSA area, which was formerly known as 'block 26', is locally known as the; "Habra Garhajis Block" which is 22,000 square kilometre.

A working petroleum system appears to be demonstrated by 9 independently verified oil seeps. Indeed, geochemical analyses of these seeps indicate a light oil or condensate that is consistent with the oils produced in Yemen which has been estimated to contain billions of barrels of oil. Jacka Resources also committed to completing a 1,500km 2D seismic survey. In addition, Ophir Energy, a London based explorer, secured exploration rights to operate in the two blocks near Berbera. DNO International, a Norway based oil firm, entered into a Production Sharing Contract covering Block SL 18 onshore in Somaliland in April 2013. Along

---

[54] http://www.thisisafricaonline.com/Business/Somaliland-set-to-drill-for-oil-by-2014?ct=true

with Sterling, it is the latest company to join the rush for black gold in Somaliland.

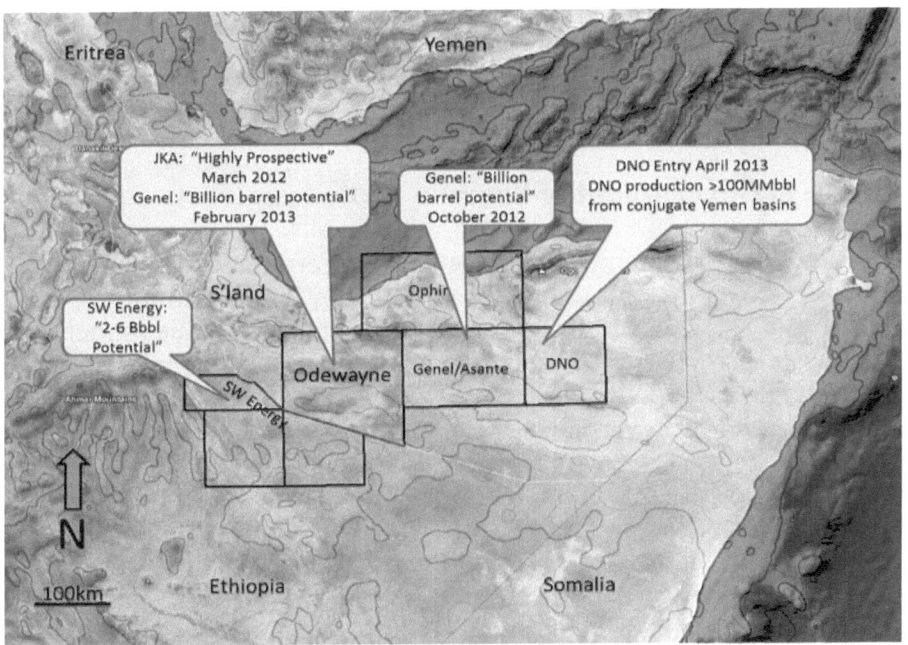

Image 5 Somaliland oil concessions

Oil concession concerns:

With Somaliland being unrecognised and lacking any concrete cooperation with the central government in Mogadishu, it has recently suffered from various obstacles in its oil exploration pursuits. Firstly, Somaliland has been criticized for offering concessions to DNO in regards to the Nugaal valley, which remains a disputed territory with Puntland and local militias. Indeed, the Puntland administration has severely condemned Somaliland for what it believes is an encroachment on its own territory and more specifically the territory it granted to Range Resources and Africa Oil, prior to the Somaliland expansion into the Sool region in 2007. However, it is important to note that the Somaliland administration also believes that this block falls under its jurisdiction.

In addition, Somaliland suffered from the public departure of Genel from its exploration activities in the Odewayne block in early

September 2013 which according to a spokesman was due to a deteriorating security situation which led them to temporarily suspending their seismic operations. However, according to the Somaliland's natural resources Minister, Genel has now to return to its activities in Somaliland as security threats have allegedly been rectified. This version of events was corroborated by CEO Tony Hayward's visit to Hargeisa in late November 2013. [55]

Federal Government of Somalia and oil exploration:

It is crucial to remember that the prior governments of Somalia were all transitional and for this reason they were institutionally weak and had little ability to grant exploration rights, due to their own security concerns and the transitional nature of their role. However, in September 2012, Somalia underwent major milestones in its governance as the new constitution was adopted, with a new parliament and President. This then enabled the central government of Somalia to move from a transitional framework to a Federal framework, enabling it to possess a degree of legitimacy amongst the international community.

In the aftermath of these developments, the new Federal Government of Somalia - under President Hassan Sheikh - has moved swiftly to entice investors to Somalia and especially its natural resources sector.

In a milestone policy statement, the central government called for renegotiations with the oil majors such as BP and Shell which declared their concessions "force majeure" in light of the civil war. In particular, the central government has highlighted that these oil majors will receive due priority. In a blow to regional aspirations to dispense oil contracts, the National Resources Minister, Abdirizak Omar Mohamed, said in a London energy conference that; *"Any contract that was given or awarded by a federal member state is not valid... foreign oil companies should start negotiations with the federal government."*

This has been the clearest indication of the policy stance of the Federal government towards oil exploration and the regional authorities and some observers have cautioned against a heightening of tensions regarding oil explorations. Indeed, the

---

[55] http://www.somalilandsun.com/index.php/economic/4360-somaliland-genel-energy-is-back-to-business

Puntland administration cut relations off with the internationally recognised Federal government due to its own belief that the central government has disregarded its autonomy. In addition, Somaliland and the central government have both continued their gradual Ankara talks and as far as reports show, there have been no negotiations between the two regarding oil exploration rights. Indeed, domestic and diaspora-led lobby groups have emerged in recent times to act as pressure groups regarding oil exploration. Principally amongst these is the East Africa Energy Forum which has as its mission statements:

- **The East African Energy Forum seeks to promote, preserve and protect the natural resources, environment and sovereignty of Somalia for current and future generations.**
- **The East African Energy Forum works to facilitate the production of a robust public policy governing the natural resources of Somalia and to educate the public on their natural resource wealth and development.**
- **The EAEF works directly with the Federal government and the natural resources ministry and thus it acts as a positive means of protecting the territorial integrity of Somalia in terms of natural resources exploration and contracts.**

The current Federal Government of Somalia is in the process of delivering a Petroleum Law that will further define aspects of natural resource ownership amongst the centre and the regions.

The central government managed to reach a landmark deal with Soma Oil & Gas, a London based company (headed by former Conservative chairman Lord Howard). They plan to invest about $20 million in the seismic research off the coast of Somalia. Indeed such an agreement proved to be monumental, as Somagas had been created solely with the intention of increasing the exploration and development of Somalia's oil and gas industry.

5. LEGAL & REGULATORY FRAMEWORK

According to development experts and the African Development Bank when developing oil and gas, an appropriate legal and regulatory framework is crucial (ADB, 2009). In Somalia's case, the first step is to initiate legal and regulatory legislation outlining the oil and gas sector which would serve to lay out a framework for the government and foreign companies to follow. The framework should also include licensing and policy matters such as profit sharing, government share, job creation, royalties, cost revenue limits, local contents such as local community development projects, training local expertise or environment issues (Oilwatch Africa, 2010).

Unfortunately, the existing legal and regulatory framework in Somalia is not clear yet and is significantly blurred between the central government and the regions. According to an article written by IRIN, the Puntland Finance Minister claimed that both the TFG and Puntland state of Somalia were working together on a legal framework relationship between the transitional federal government and Puntland government. Also in the past there has been a discussion on national hydrocarbon law, which was developed by the previous TFG. The reason why such legislation is needed is to counter corruption. For example, "*...according to Transparency International, oil and gas producing countries in Africa are among the most corrupted in the world. For example out of 178 countries. Chad ranks at 171, Angola at 168, Nigeria 134, Libya 146 and Algeria 105... Somalia is ranked at 178.*"

The previous TFG government planned to adopt a production sharing agreement (PSA) contract law and also named its national oil and gas company, Somalia Petroleum Company (SPC). In this regard it was a good start, however, like many policies under the beleaguered TFG, it never came to fruition. Speaking prior to the adoption of the draft constitution, a Puntland Minster said the draft constitution, which was completed in September 2012 "*...will make it clear how the resources will be shared*".

The advent of Somalia's Federal Government and natural resources regulation:

With the end of the transitional period for Somalia's government and the advent of the Federal Government and the Hassan Sheikh

Presidency, Somalia gained a considerable degree of stability and international recognition. This in turn provided the Somali central government with increased international assistance, collaboration and increased ownership of their own resources. This led to the Federal government seeking to exploit Somalia's own natural resources to accelerate development, which included inviting major, foreign oil companies to return to Somalia and drill.

The Somali Petroleum Law was enacted in 2008 by the previous Transitional Federal Government. Aspects of its regulations are not stringent enough and are open to different interpretations by the Federal government, regional authorities as well as oil companies. For example, one article states that any Oil and Gas agreement should be signed by both Federal and regional governments. Yet this has caused more confusion as there still has not been a defined constitutional separation of ownership between the regions and the centre. As a result, when the law does not separate clearly the federal authority and local government, a legal battle might erupt under the rally cries of "federalism", "regionalism" or "constitutional rights".

In a nutshell, the Somali Petroleum Law needs to be revised and harmonized in the hydrocarbon sector, including legal, technical and commercial aspects. The current Federal Government of Somalia is still in the process of delivering this awaited Petroleum Law that will further define aspects of natural resource ownership amongst the centre and the regions. This is because there has been some confusion regarding the independence of regional authorities such as Puntland and Somaliland - who have been vigorously granting their own contracts, thus bypassing the central government.

6. ECONOMIC OPPORTUNITIES OF OIL & GAS EXPLORATION

Development:
Some would argue that the advantages of an oil and gas boom in Somalia would be tremendous and serve as a multiplier effect on the general economy. In particular, the economic "Trickle down" argument is used to argue that oil and gas revenues will act as a multiplier effect on the economy serving to boost employment and government budgets. Somalia is plagued by extremely high levels of unemployment and an exponential rise in oil exploration and oil

drilling can provide countless job creation opportunities for its citizenry. These job opportunities could then vary from skilled to unskilled labour, which will in turn provide local Somalis and diaspora Somalis with increased opportunities in this industry. For this to hold true, it is crucial that the central government of Somalia negotiates contracts with majors to ensure that the majority of the labour force are drawn from these local communities in which oil exploration is taking place.

In particular, these oil revenues can then be used to increase budget spending on education and healthcare within Somalia. Oil and gas rich states such as, Norway and Ghana, have all successfully implemented policies that have seen their resource export industry lead to economic growth with benefits trickling down to citizens. They have also, in the process, avoided the dreaded resource curse. Furthermore, sound economic policies & institutions can enable states to avoid the 'resource curse' and thus a major recommendation for the Somalia Federal Government would be to reform and develop stronger, resilient institutions.

Another positive of oil and gas revenues includes the modernisation of the agricultural sector through increased investment which will increase productivity. In a state with a populace so heavily dependent on agriculture, it would prove to be an economic lifeline for millions in Somalia. In addition, substantial oil revenues in Somalia would enable the central government to increase the levels of taxation, which is critical as it provides governments with a sound reserve base to fund developments. A government that can raise revenue via taxation is more likely to not engage in rent-seeking behaviour and will also be more likely to be held accountable by its citizens.

Potential disadvantages of natural resources:

A particular disadvantage facing developing states with an abundance of natural resources includes, the notion of the "Resource Curse" a term first coined by Richard Aunty (1993) to describe the paradoxical situation whereby resource rich states were able to boost their economies through natural resources, whilst still experiencing lower long run economic growth than non-resource rich states and increased volatility. This is because countries with abundant resources may mismanage reserves, which leads to increased rent-seeking activities from elites and a skewed distribution of wealth, which causes instability as evidenced by the ongoing issues in the Niger Delta. Indeed, Somalia being a post-conflict state is arguably at an even more precarious situation with regards to its natural resources management, especially when independent regional administrations are factored in.

When looking at research into such issues its clear that many oil rich African states such as, Angola and Nigeria, have suffered from problems linked to resource export and revenue transparency. Instead, African oil rich states have suffered from destabilising factors including conflict, corruption and authoritarianism, which were all principally a symptom of weak institutions. In Somalia's case, its lack of sufficient infrastructure may prevent it from fully capturing the advantages of oil resources. Also, with caution, economists have noted how resource abundance in the form of oil and gas usually leads to a lack of accountability and representation due to the prioritisation of oil revenues instead of tax revenues. The increased corruption linked to this resource curse then further erodes real chances of long-term growth; entrenching greater inequality and a rise in human-rights violations.

The term "Rentier States" has been used by development economists to refer to states such as, the Congo, which is reliant on the export of mineral wealth and resources. Despite this abundance of resources, their people continue to experience low per capita income and are seen as 'rentier economies'. Development economists who warn against dependency on natural resources, often cite the sensational economic development of the 'East Asian 'Tigers' which lacked any exportable natural resources but yet achieved high levels of economic growth and high living standards. This in turn poses the crucial question of whether the focus on credible institutions should precede any natural resource extraction. Another issue regarding natural resources that development economists often point to, includes the "Dutch Disease" scenario whereby the discovery of oil and gas leads to a price boom which in turn leads to the real appreciation of currency and simultaneously the crowding out of growth to manufacturing sectors. In the long run, this has negative economic ramifications because the technical progress linked to manufacturing has slowed down considerably.

According to notable development economists such as, Collier & Hoeffler (2004), the abundance of natural resources often leads to increased instances of conflict and the neglect of economic and institutional reforms crucial to economic development. Thus to fully benefit from natural resources, developing states such as Somalia should focus on developing credible institutions which serve as effective checks and balances against corruption and inefficiency. A key example of an African state with sound institutions and considerable natural wealth (in the form of diamonds) is Botswana which has experienced consistent economic growth and human development in the past few decades.

7. NATURAL RESOURCES AND THE ENVIRONMENT

The infrastructure and expertise needed to develop a modern oil and gas sector is considerable and currently beyond the reach of a post-conflict state such as, Somalia. Nevertheless, the central government should ensure that it addresses the environmental issues that may arise out of oil exploration to the various communities concerned. Because most of the oil explorations throughout the country, from North to South, occur in the coastal regions, it is no surprise to find that it is often rural communities that will be affected environmentally. Indeed, Somalia already has a history of falling victim to foreign environmental degradation such as the infamous toxic dumping off its coast. Therefore, to overcome such issues it is incumbent upon the government to develop its institutions and regulatory framework, as well as meeting international standards and treaties. Extreme cases such as the April 20th 2010 BP Gulf of Mexico oil spill disaster show the catastrophic damage such a sector could have on the local environment. The fallout from the large oil spill served to negatively impact the fishing community, tourism industry and the biodiversity in the area. What is most worrying for African states seeking to benefit from the natural resources sector is that, despite BP being an oil major, a lack of safety procedures and poor communications were identified as key causes of the disaster. Other such disasters caused by oil and gas activities include, the 1984 Bhopal chemical industry in India which leaked poison gas and killed thousands of local people. This is all relevant because a state such as, Somalia - with a fragile economy and poor infrastructure, will suffer disproportionately should there occur any environmental disasters. This is because response units, resources, fund and expertise are needed, which Somalia does not currently possess.

In a best practice approach, the International oil companies (IOCs) should finance a local or international fund that can be mobilised in case of local environmental disasters. In the case of Somalia where oil exploration is currently ongoing, this could prove to be prudent.

8. SUMMARY

- **Things can only continue to improve in Somalia and, in 2007, the Federal Government of Nigeria set itself the target of reaching 7% renewable energy by 2025.**

- **Although in its formative stages, the central government needs to place major emphasis on renewable energy promotion as it will act as a future creator of jobs - and it will become a major form of energy provision. Monopolistic electricity firms in urban Somali cities should be countered by the central government. These electric energy firms managed to thrive under the lack of a regulatory environment, however, they have also negatively impacted average citizens through steep rises in prices and inefficient services. I believe that a taskforce should negotiate with these monopolistic electricity firms in order to set a planned price which will enable the majority of citizens to benefit from electricity and not just the middle classes as is the current arrangement.**

- **I am looking forward to the day when renewable energy sectors thrive in Somalia. Also, it is well-known that Somalia is projected to become a potential oil producing state and it's no surprise to see that foreign oil companies have already signed oil exploration contracts with the central government and regional administrations. In the long-term, similar to the policy long adopted by Nigeria, the central government could provide fuel and energy subsidies based on this oil potential. This in turn will enable the citizenry to be able to better afford energy services throughout Somalia.**

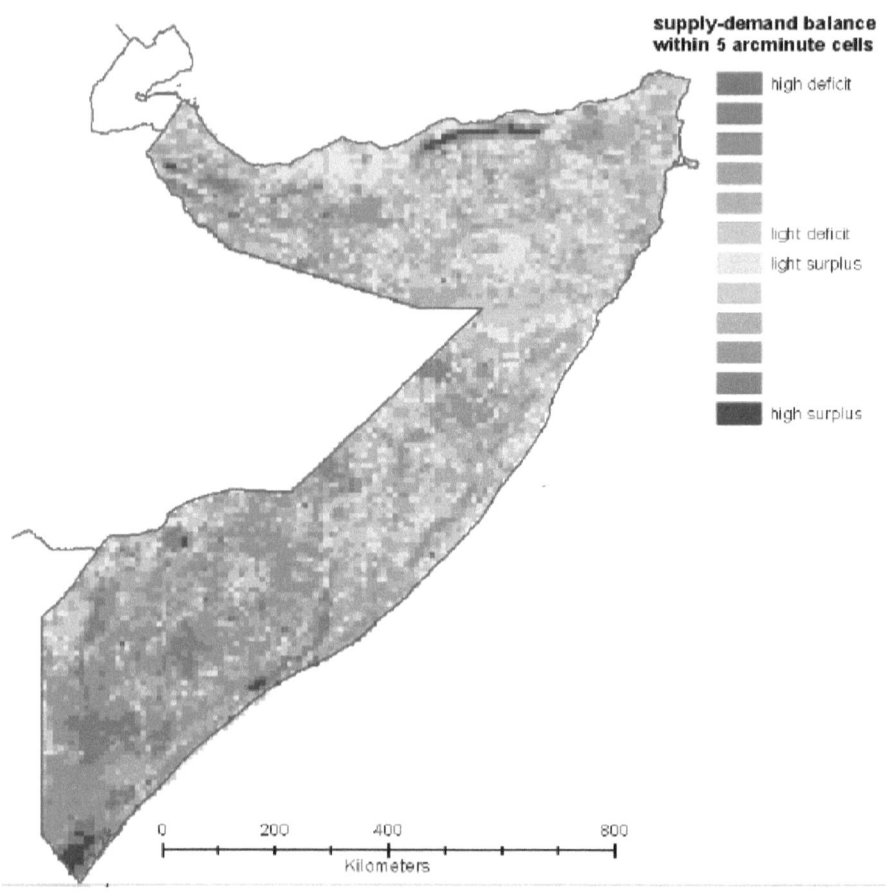

Map :- 1 : Biomass, wood and fuel consumption in Somalia. Supply & Demand in rural and urban centres.1

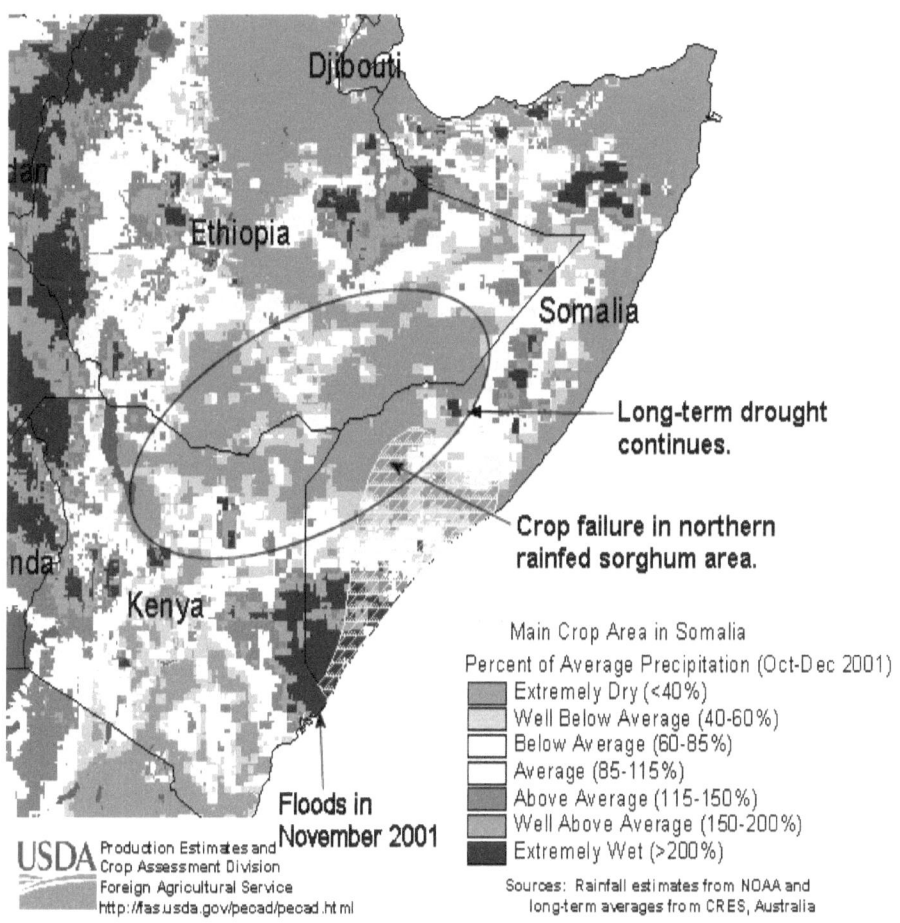

Map :- 2 highlighting water scarcity within Somalia

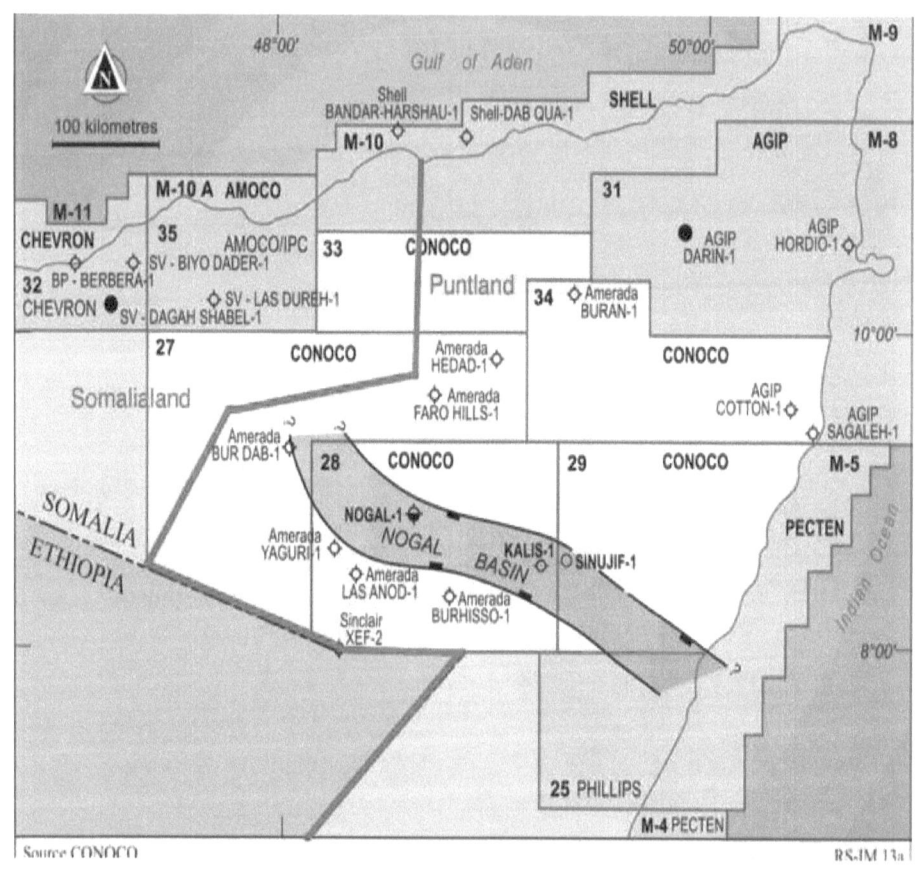

Old concessions awarded to Majors by the Siad Barre government.

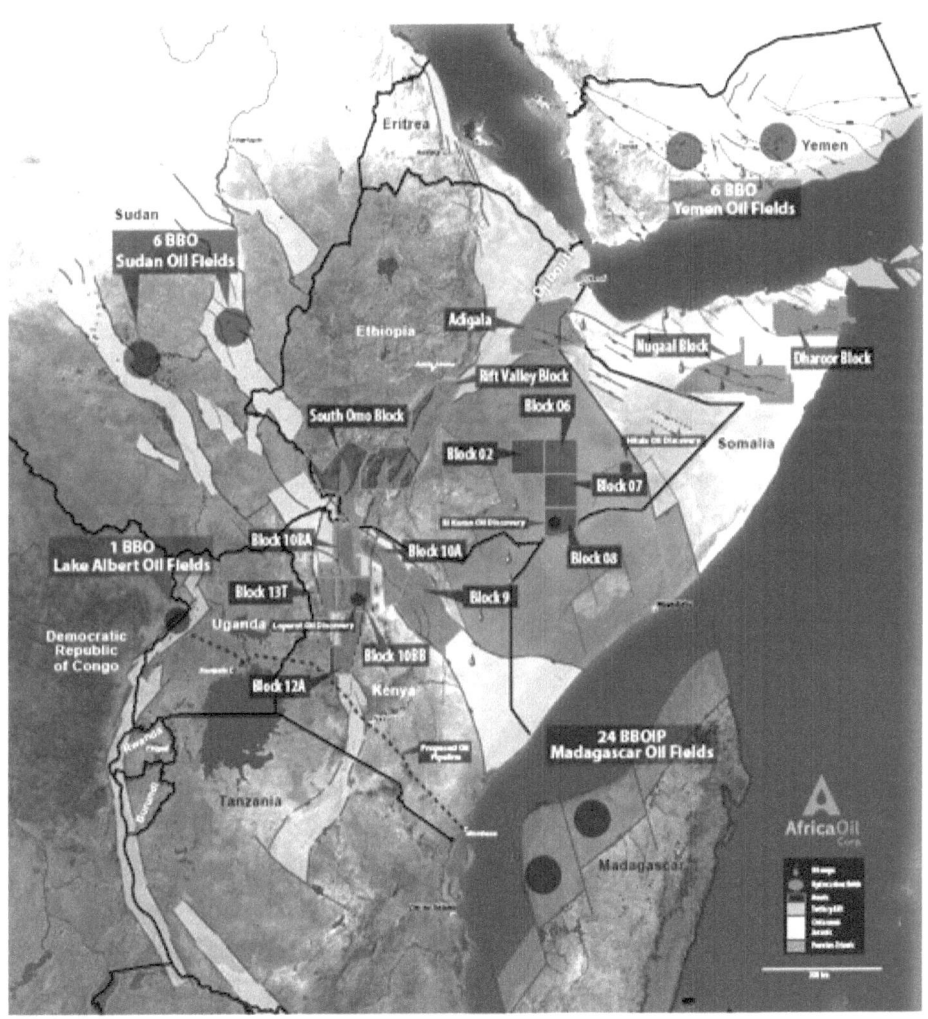

Current Oil exploration in the Horn of Africa.

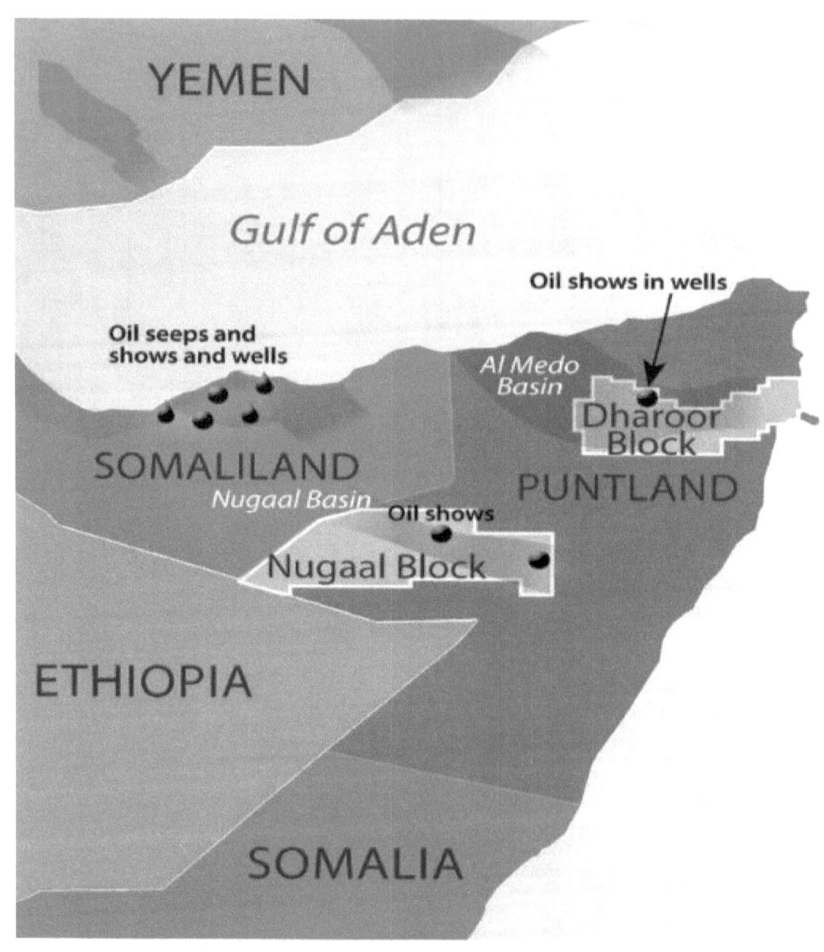

Oil exploration in Puntland and Somaliland.

CHAPTER FIVE

INFRASTRUCTURE

Introduction:

One of the main objectives of the Somali Economic Forum has always been to promote sustainable economic development in Somalia and central to this is the development of infrastructure.

Infrastructural development is critical for an economy to function and can therefore be defined as the set of interconnected structural elements that provide a framework for conducive economic development. It is this objective that has led to us formulating this infrastructure report which involved conducting in-depth economic research on the infrastructure already existing within Somalia and the infrastructure needs of Somalia as a state.

The main purpose of the chapter is to primarily convey the infrastructure already prevalent in Somalia such as: road networks, airports, seaports etc. However, a secondary objective of ours was to enable the wider public to learn about the burgeoning infrastructure sector in Somalia and to provide potential foreign and domestic investors with the necessary knowledge of Somalia's infrastructure - in order to facilitate foreign and domestic investment.

In addition, I hope that this chapter will encourage potential investors, whether foreign or domestic, to invest in Somalia's infrastructure which we believe will yield high returns in the long run.

I believe that increased efficiency and investment in Somalia's infrastructure will help to transform Somalia rapidly in terms of its economy.

Crucially, with the prominence of Public Private Partnerships (PPPs) in recent decades, I have dedicated a portion of this chapter to economic benefits and applicability of PPPs in the context of Somalia, which already benefits from high rates of diaspora investment.

1. Infrastructure in Soalia

Overview of infrastructure within Somalia:

When discussing the infrastructure of Somalia, it is crucial to remember that Somalia has just emerged from a two decade civil war which has led to destroyed or deteriorating infrastructure which has seen little improvement in the last decade. Indeed, prior to the civil war in 1991, Somalia was seen as an African example in terms of infrastructure development and state-led investment in the sector, as the state benefited from extensive road networks, efficient airports and ports that acted as the economic lifeline to the Somali state.

Infrastructure in economic terminology is usually a public good which requires a strong central government to administer, something Somalia has lacked for two decades and this in part explains the stagnation in Somalia's infrastructural sector in recent decades, however, there have been successes in this domain.

In terms of roads within Somalia, currently one paved road extends from Berbera in the North, all the way through to Mogadishu and Kismayo in the South. Road networks of all categories total to approx. 27,600 kilometres of which only 3,608 kilometres is paved. In addition to these paved roads there are a substantial number of dirt roads - roads that have been created - and these types of roads are usually found in rural and coastal areas. Many of these improved earth roads are frequently impassable during rainy seasons. Another issue that we will touch on in later in our report is road infrastructure and how these road networks are acutely insufficient when trying to open up isolated areas or to link specific regions.

Furthermore, in terms of its airports, Somalia has 8 paved civilian airfields and fewer than 20 additional widely scattered gravel airfields in various districts and regions.

The international airport of Somalia is based in its capital city, Mogadishu. In 1990, a domestic service linked Mogadishu with 7 other Somali cities served, in part, by Somali Airlines, which owned 1 Airbus 310 in 1989. With the advent of the civil war in 1992, all scheduled domestic services ceased and only began to pick up pace in the late 1990s.

In terms of its electrical infrastructure, usually electricity is produced entirely from diesel and petrol powered generators, with all the fuel imported. In 1998, it was estimated that 265 million kilowatt hours (kWh) were supplied, all from privately-owned generators. There is some hydroelectric potential on Somalia's rivers, but thus far it has remained unexploited and is likely to remain so, until Somalia's security and stability are better established. Poor people, and most of the population outside the towns, rely on wood for cooking and kerosene oil lamps for light.

There are 4 major ports located within Somalia and those with deep-water facilities include ports based at Berbera, Mogadishu, and Kismaayo and a lighterage (for transportation of goods on flat-bottomed barges) port at Marka (plus, a minor port at Maydh). A port modernisation program that was launched in the latter half of 1980s with U.S. aid, significantly improved cargo handling capabilities at Kismaayo and increased the number of berths and deepened the harbour at Berbera - which currently benefits from the distinction of being one of the deepest seaports in East Africa.

Somalia's public telecommunications system was completely destroyed or dismantled during the civil war by various factions; all relief organisations depended on their own private communication systems. However, in the past decade, local telecommunication systems have emerged and established themselves throughout urban cities and centres such as: Mogadishu, Hargeisa, Garowe and in several other urban centres. These Somali-owned telecommunication firms provide some of the most innovative and cheapest telecommunication services in Africa.

In terms of Somalia's domestic economy, telecommunication firms have no doubt proved to be a major success story and it is now commonplace for people to make international connections from their mobile phones or call centres in Somalia.

Relative to our discussion on Somalia's infrastructure, these major telecommunication firms have often assumed the role of the government and built telecommunication towers and the related infrastructure.

With the collapse of Siad Barre's regime in 1991, there emerged a lack of any genuine, effective centralized government in control of

Somalia. Indeed, this trend was only arrested in recent years with the election of Somalia's current President Hassan M. Sheikh in September 2012. Unsurprisingly, the instability over the years has resulted in the neglect of Somalia's infrastructure with roads, airports, seaports, bridges and hospitals all deteriorating in condition over time.

Investment is needed in logistical infrastructure to improve the ability of construction development to occur across the country. The main transportation infrastructures in Somalia include roads, seaports and airports. However, there are no railways, pipelines or inland waterways. The transportation infrastructure and public transportation system currently existing in Somalia is very limited and heavily privatised, with a lack of development or modernisation over the past two decades.

At Independence in the early 1960s, Somalia inherited an underdeveloped roads network system consisting of a few paved roads in the urban centres in the South and Northwest, as well as four undeveloped ports, equipped only with lighterage facilities, and a handful of usable airstrips.

During the next three decades, some improvements in infrastructure were made with the help of substantial levels of donor funds and foreign aid. Yet, it is crucial to note that prior to the civil war - and even in the aftermath of it - there still existed primary, all-weather roads connecting most of the important towns which linked the Northern and Southern parts of the country.

During this interim period; there has been the modernisation of three ports which have been substantially improved, along with eight airports that have paved runways, and regular domestic air service was also established and maintained. But in early 1992, the country still lacked the necessary roads infrastructure to open up undeveloped areas or to link isolated regions, and shipping had come to a virtual halt because of the security situation at the time.

The general infrastructure of Somalia includes approximately 26,000 km of roads (of which 3,200 km were paved, 3,500 KM are gravel and the rest is improved earth), four major ports, and fifteen major airfields, seven of which have paved runways.

Since the late 1980s, only 12 percent of paved road networks have been refurbished and developed. Finally, the capital infrastructure stock that Somalia had built up by the late 1980s, has been largely depleted.

1.1 Roads

Somalia's principal highway was a 1,886 kilometre (1,172 miles) two-lane paved road that runs from Kismayo in the South through Mogadishu and all the way to Hargeisa and Berbera in the North.

Map :- 3 Somalia (South – North Road)

This route ran inland, roughly paralleling the border with Ethiopia. Somalia's 1988 plan provided for another connection from this main route to Boosaaso on the Gulf of Aden.

Somalia had only one paved road that extended from north of Mogadishu to Ethiopia; all other links to neighbouring countries were dirt trails which were often closed during the rainy seasons.

A 750 km highway connects major cities in the Northern parts of the country, such as Bosaso, Galkayo, and Garowe, with towns in the south.

In 2012, the Puntland Highway Authority (PHA) completed rehabilitation work on the central road artery linking Garowe with Galkayo. The PHA body also began an upgrade and repair project in June 2012 on the large thoroughfare between Bosaso and Garowe. Additionally, renovations were initiated in October 2012 on the central artery linking Bosaso with Qardho. Plans are also in the works to construct new roads connecting littoral towns in the region to the main road networks to Garowe and the commercial city of Bosaso.

Puntland alone has 900KM of tarmac road connecting Bosaso, the port city on the gulf shore at the northern end to Galkayo, the southern end. There is also an extensive network of rough feeder roads connecting the remote towns, villages, coastal settlements, and inland rural areas to tarmac roads located in towns. Puntland Highway Authorities agency is responsible for building and repairing the Puntland Roads and they have undertaken several initiatives to build and repair the damages caused by rains and heavy trucks.

In the Somaliland region, the main roads found in the cities of Hargeisa, Berbera and Burao still consist of the roads built during the Siad Barre era and especially the Hargeisa-Sheikh-Berbera mountainside road network which was built by Chinese engineers in the 1970s. In modern times, the Somaliland Road Development Agency oversees the development and maintenance of roads with the region. According to the Somaliland RDA, the current "administration adopts a participatory approach in which diaspora communities in collaboration with the government take part in the construction of road development projects."[56]

Examples of such private and public investment in the development of road networks include, Dawga-Cad Road, which serves to link Hargeisa to the coastal and sub-coastal areas below

---

[56] http://somalilandroads.com/Projects/Index

the Golis Mountains of Bulahar, Eilsheikh, Lughaya and Zeila. Moreover, the construction of a multimillion pound fully tarmacked 400 KM road connecting Erigavo, Burao, Las Qoray has recently begun. The road, which begins from Ina Afmadoobe village, east of Burao, will connect the Las Anod to Burao tarmac road - built by the Chinese in the Seventies to Erigavo through the Saraar plateau. This initiative was long overdue and acts as a means to connect the notoriously inaccessible Sanaag regions with larger towns and cities in the northern region. It is expected to significantly boost trade, commerce and economic development particularly in the less developed but aesthetically stunning Sanaag region. Such a project has gained widespread publicity, due to the burden of the costs falling on the diaspora communities who have pledged around $7.5million to the Erigavo road.

In addition, many of the roads within the Somaliland region have been mostly diaspora-funded projects including, the current Borama-Dilla road constituted in the Somaliland region. Also, there has recently been a fundraising drive initiated by the diaspora of the Burao/Erigavo communities to construct a road connecting the Toghdeer region with the isolated Sanaag region.

With Mogadishu undergoing an economic and political revival, it has seen the most investment in road networks in recent years. These improvements have been led by Turkish investors and the Turkish Investment Agency, which aims to establish Mogadishu and Istanbul as twin cities and rebuild most of Mogadishu's roads to international standards. An example can be found in the 23km paved road, linking Mogadishu international airport to the city centre. In addition, the vast majority of Mogadishu's main central roads have been refurbished along with solar street lamps being constructed to provide further security. With Mogadishu being the capital and undergoing rapid economic revival, it is logical that it has the highest inter-city road network of all the Somali cities, which is only expected to grow due to large international and domestic investment in the roads.

In September 2013, the Somali federal government signed an official cooperation agreement with its Chinese counterpart in Mogadishu as part of a five-year national recovery plan.

The pact will see the Chinese authorities reconstruct several major infrastructural landmarks in the Somali capital and elsewhere, as well as the road between Galkayo and Burao in the Northern part of the country.

The lack of road infrastructure is presently still a major issue, in, for instance: Middle Shabelle, Galgaduud, Mudug, Nugaal and Bari. These coastal regions are only linked by dirt roads. As such, they lack accessibility which has exacerbated insecurity issues, with bandits taking advantage of the poor isolated roads to set up checkpoints and steal from passers-by. Indeed, prior to the civil war, these coastal regions were difficult to reach and the following two decades civil war has only exacerbated the inaccessible nature of these areas via roads.

Thus, investment is required to build roads linking the Southern coastal regions to cities such as: Mogadishu, Cadale, Ceeldheer, Xarardheere, Hobyo, Garacad, Eyl, and Bandarbeyla to Caluula - which would boost the regional economic development, as well as creating employment for the local communities.

The most isolated and affected areas have no proper road infrastructures, except some sand and gravel roads. Proposal roads can be invested in to help bring about much needed regional development. For example, building a main road from Mogadishu going through the whole coast regions and other connection branches between the main road, offshore cities, districts and regions will benefit the whole region.

Road transport continues to be the principal mode of internal transport due to a lack of railway infrastructure and limited coastal shipping.

Although, the Somalia road network has undergone vast improvements, much of the roads in the country have been rated as been sub-standard.

The country's road network undoubtedly has a reasonable amount of good sections, however this represents a fraction in what is otherwise a below par national roads system. This is largely due to the previous years of internal strife, as well as the lack of investment by authorities, who for all their efforts are working within the current funding constraints to upgrade the treacherous stretches of roads which are still quite common.

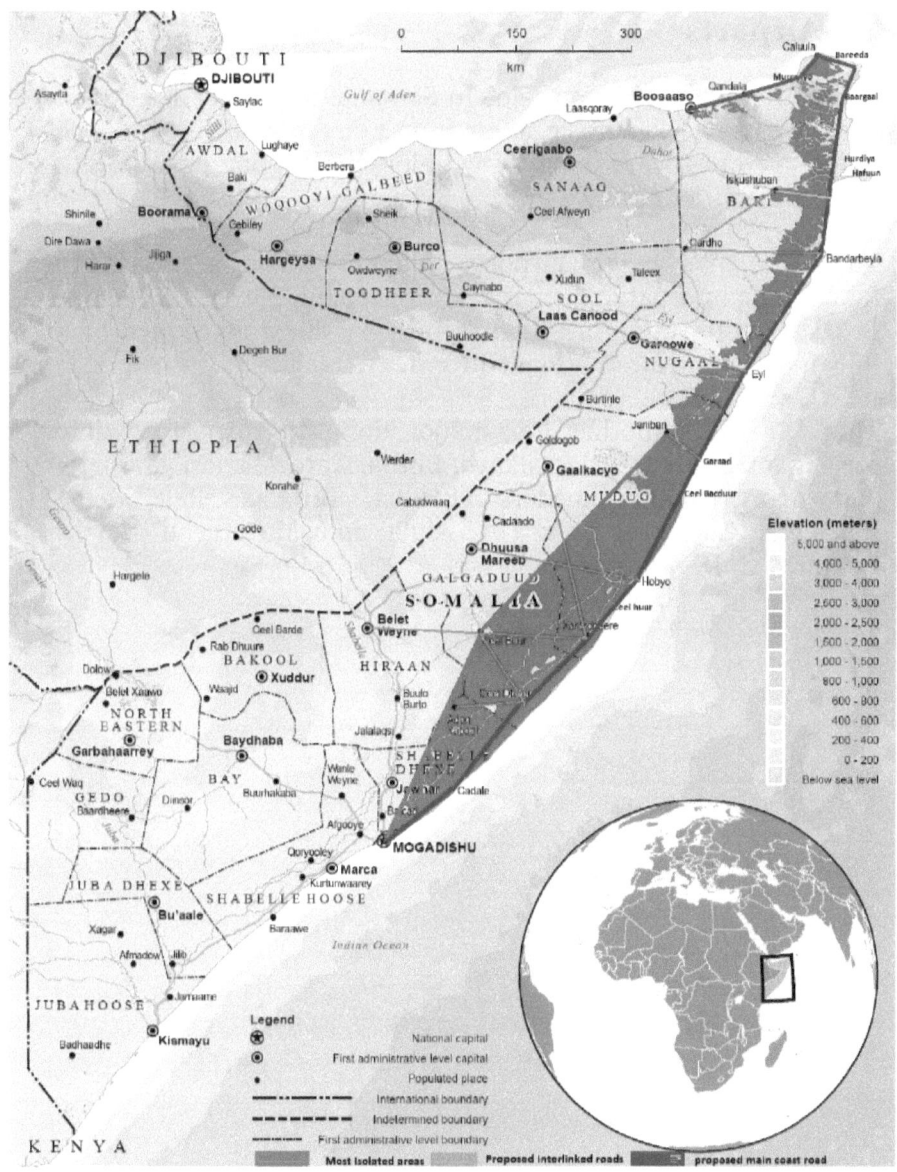

Figure 5.2: Somalia Map of unpaved road networks and isolated areas

1.2 Airports

There are a total of 62 airfields in Somalia, of which 7 are paved and have runway lengths ranging from 1,524 to 3,047 meters. The other 55 runways are unpaved with lengths ranging from 900 to 3,047meters.

There are five major airports, four of which are partially functioning international airports (Mogadishu, Berbera, Kismayo, Bosaso) while Hargeisa's Egal Airport has been accredited as a fully functioning international airport.

There are also another four major domestic airports mainly serving intrastate travel (Galkayo, Buroa, Garowe and Ballidogle) and many smaller feeders (Baidoa, Borama, Beledweyne Bardhere, Garoowe, Kalabayd, Alula and Mogadishu North-Dayniile, etc).

Due to the insecurity of travelling in Somalia, particularly in the many isolated and volatile regions, there are numerous small airstrips in development including: Jowhar, Mareray, Garbahare, Luuq, Taleex, Afmadow, Wajid in Bakool, Saakow and Bu'aale in middle Juba, Jamame in lower Juba, Abudwaq in Galguduud, and several others in Galgudud such as Ceelbuur, Guriceel and Cadaado.

In the last few years, the private sector has opened up new international routes within Somalia and this has been a growing trend. In order to meet international standards, rehabilitation work needs to begin in the aforementioned airports, as well as: Garowe, Beledweyne, Baidoa and Bosaso airports.

Air transportation is provided by up to 14 Somali-owned airline firms operating 62 aircraft, offering commercial flights to international locations, the more popular domestic air carriers are: Jubba Airways, Daallo Airlines and Puntair.

More recently, international airline carriers such as Turkish Airlines, Ethiopian Airlines and African Express have, among others, extended their operations to Somalia.

In fact, Turkish Airlines became the first long-distance international commercial airline in two decades to land at Mogadishu's Aden Adde International Airport. As of March 2012, the flag carrier now offers two flights a week from the Somali capital to Istanbul.

There are also 55 domestic airstrips providing limited passenger and freight services.

Figure 1 Runway Length of Paved Airports in Somalia

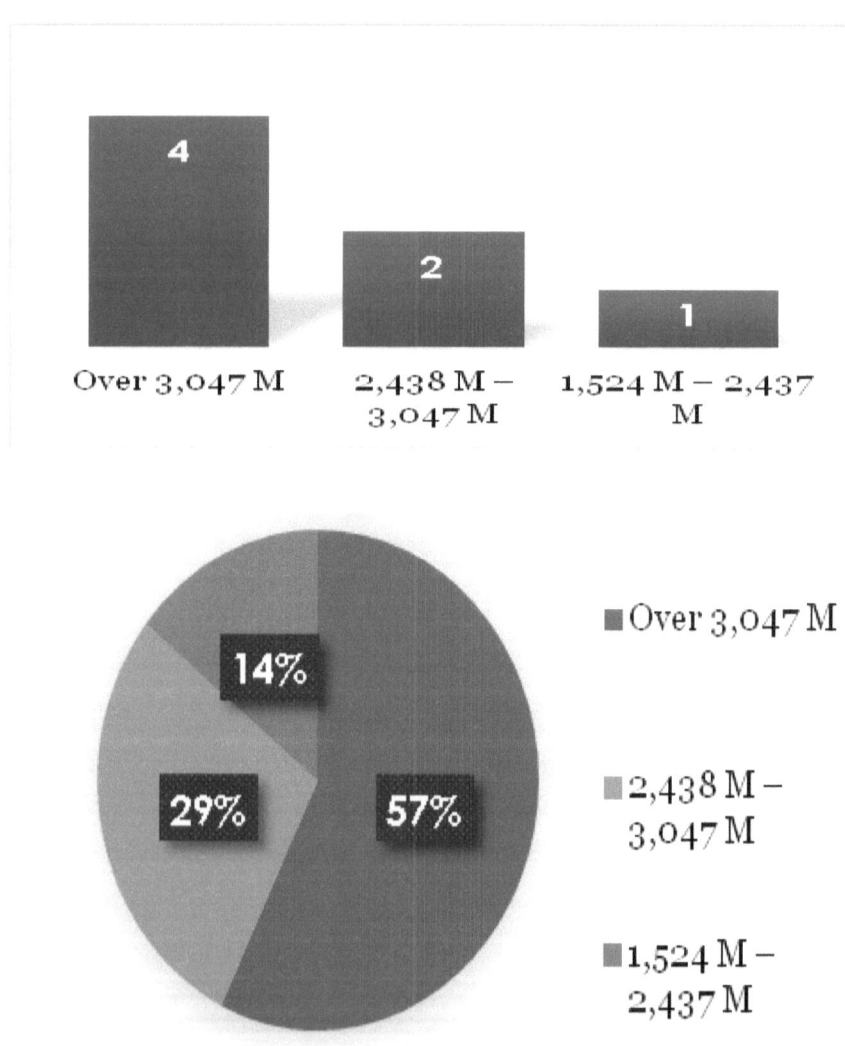

Fig 5.4. Runway Length of Unpaved Airports in Somalia

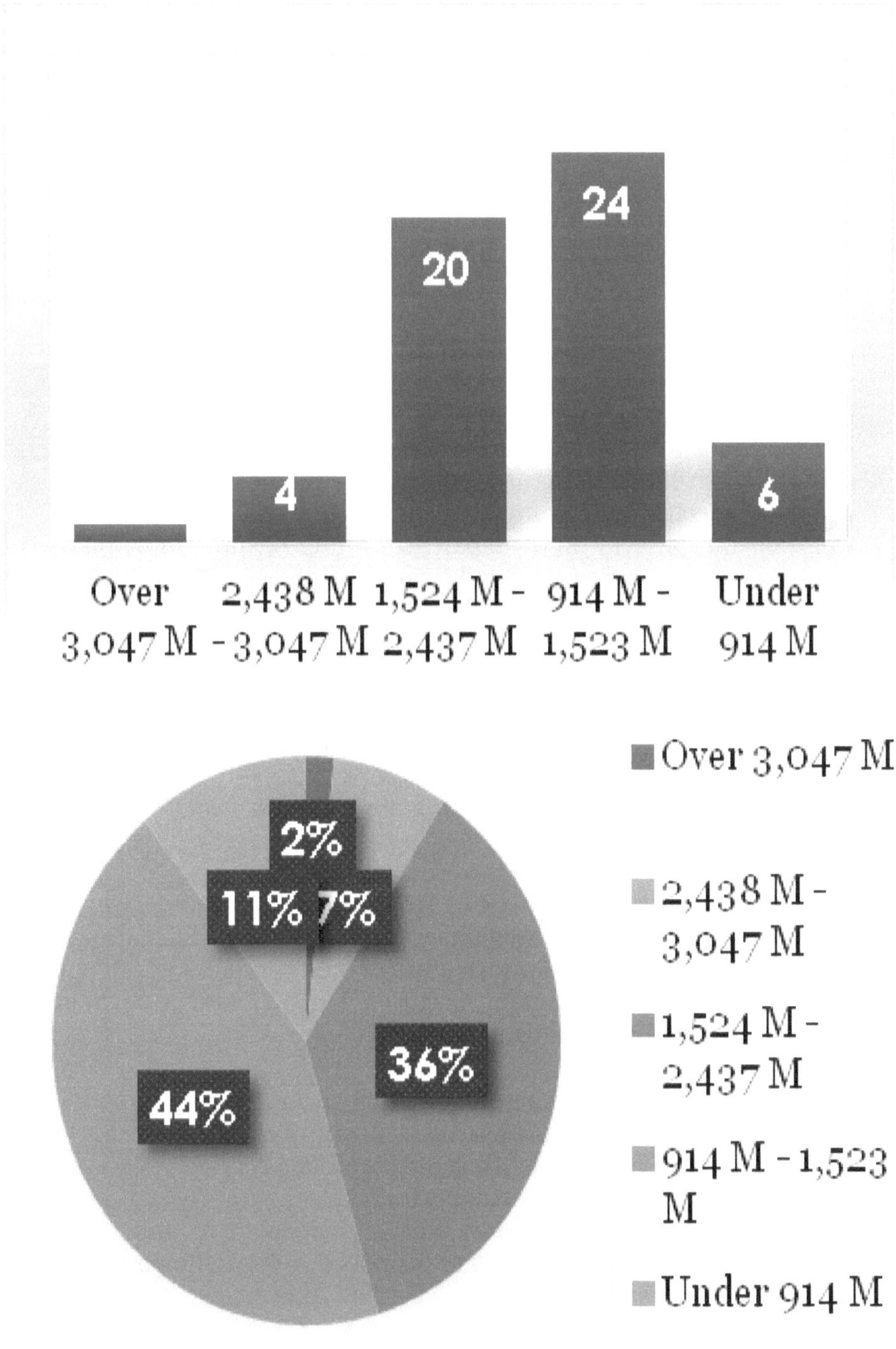

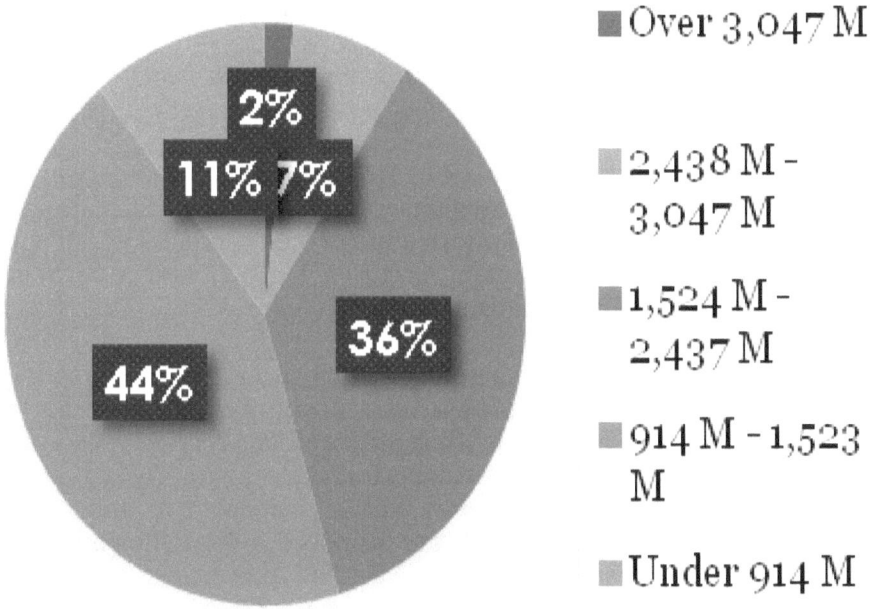

Mogadishu Aden Adde International Airport: In late 2010, SKA Air and Logistics, a Dubai-based aviation firm that specializes in conflict zones, was contracted by the Somali government to manage operations over a period of ten years at the re-opened Aden Adde International Airport. With concurrent activities in Iraq and Afghanistan, among other complex areas, the company was assigned the task of running security screening, passenger security and terminals. The Ministry of Transport officially announced the partnership in May 2011, with the domestically registered firm SKA-Somalia starting operations in July of the year.

Among its first initiatives, worth an estimated $6 million, SKA invested in new airport equipment and expanded support services by hiring, training and equipping 200 local workers to meet international airport standards. The company also assisted in comprehensive infrastructure renovations, restored a dependable supply of electricity, revamped the baggage handling facilities as well as the arrival and departure lounges, put into place electronic check-in systems, and firmed up on security and workflow. Additionally, SKA connected the grounds' Somali Civil Aviation and Meteorological Agency (SCAMA) and immigration, customs, commercial airlines and Somali Police Force officials to the Internet. By January 2013, the firm had introduced shuttle buses to ferry travellers to and from the passenger terminal. It is also providing consultancy on support services in other airports around the country, and investing in logistical redevelopment solutions.

However, on September 15th 2013 Mogadishu airport underwent a transition in airport management from Dubai-based SKA air and logistics to Favori LLC a Turkish state-owned company which will provide increased investment, security, logistics and a 24-hour service throughout Mogadishu airport. [57]

In the past year Mogadishu airport has succeeded in attracting ever-larger aircraft to its refurbished runways, for example a Boeing 747-281F ER-BBS landing at Mogadishu Airport runway in August 2013. With the recent investment deal with Turkish state firm Favori Mogadishu, airport will be scheduled to undergo a multimillion investment with the proposed format shown in the image below.

---

[57] http://sabahionline.com/en_GB/articles/hoa/articles/features/2013/09/05/feature-01

- Figure 5.5: Favori Artists' impression of Mogadishu International Airport in 2016

Hargeisa Egal International Airport: The Somaliland region's main airport had undergone construction from early 2012 until August 2013, due to funding from the Kuwait Fund for Arab Economic Development which totalled $10 million, with half allocated to Hargeisa airport and the remaining amount allocated to Berbera airport. The investment in Hargeisa airport served to enlarge the runway by 1.6km to accommodate larger aircraft, add two new terminals and five wind turbines, along with a wind data monitoring centre to assist in powering the airport.

In September 1, Ethiopian Airlines inaugurated a B737 service to Hargeisa airport's newly extended 2.4km runway.[58] However, a couple of weeks later, Ethiopian Airlines cancelled flights to Hargeisa due to its concern over the state of the runway renovation which has thrown into doubt the efficiency of the reconstruction. However, as of January 2014, Hargeisa Egal International Airport is now up and running again, which has in turn enabled increased flights to and from the airport.

---

[58] http://www.routes-news.com/news/1-news/1806-somaliland-chases-air-links-in-campaign-for-nationhood

In contrast, Berbera airport has always accommodated large aircrafts such as those used by Ethiopian Airlines; mainly due to it having one of the longest runways in Africa – after investment from the former USSR under the Siad Barre regime. In addition, under the Cold War politics of the 1980s, Siad Barre managed to solicit funding from the USA - which enabled the Berbera runway to be enlarged and be the emergency landing point for the NASA shuttle project.

The investments in Berbera airport have led to a new terminal and 16km of security fencing, improved screening and baggage facilities.

Bosaso Bender Qassim International Airport: Within the Puntland State of Somalia, there has been a constant push to modernise and significantly enlarge Bosaso Airport and turn it into a major hub within the region. Bosaso Airport (also named The Bender Qassim International Airport) is the third-largest airport in Somalia after Mogadishu and Hargeisa airports, respectively. It has recently received funding from Italy and UNPOS to enlarge the runway. In late September 2013, a launch of the tender process for the Bosaso Airport's renovations was held. It was attended by Puntland government officials and aviation officials, as well as representatives of around 20 international companies, with over 24 firms vying for the project. [59]

1.3 Ports

Somalia has one of the largest coastlines in Africa, which measures around 3300 km. The country has some of the biggest and busiest ports in the entire East African region.

There are four major ports in Somalia: Bosaso, Berbera, Mogadishu and Kismayo - and they fall under the jurisdiction of separate Somali Ports Authorities who control and oversee operations.

In terms of the composition of the ports, only those in: Mogadishu, Berbera and Kismayo, are thus far classified as deep-water ports. In spite of this, Bosaso, is the fastest growing port in Somalia, a centre for commerce - and the Puntland authorities are seeking

---

[59] http://ilaysnews.net/2013/09/somalia-20-companies-compete-for-Bosaso-airport-runway-bid/

investment with the view to modernise it so it could become a deep-water port in the near future.

Along with the four major seaports, there are various smaller ports that also handle: ships, commerce, fisheries, import and exports, although on a smaller scale. These smaller ports include: Maydh, Merca, Las Qorey and El Ma'an, etc. The aforementioned ports generally fall under independent port authorities set up by local communities, as do the smaller ports such as El Ma'an and Merca.

Due to civil instability of the past two decades, the port of Mogadishu has only recently become fully operational, although the port was still used by some private commercial operators - most avoided it for other safer ports i.e. Bosaso and Berbera. However, now that Mogadishu port has regained full operation and with expansion plans to develop its capacity by 2015, the port's future yields are promising. Mogadishu port may prove to be an economic lifeline in terms of revenue generation for the Somali Federal Government which is seeking to build and expand institutions throughout the country.

Bosasso Port: Puntland state of Somalia has several natural ports that can be used seasonally, but the only permanent port facility is the Port of Bosaso, which is arguably the busiest and most active of all the ports in Somalia. It consists of one (roll-on-roll-off) berth 175m long with a draught of 12m at high tide and 8m at low tide.

The Port Authority charges service fees for transit-goods to neighbouring countries and the Ministry of Finance charges a small tax on goods destined for local consumption. The Puntland government plans to enlarge Bosaso port, a key source of government revenue through taxation, imports and exports at one of Somalia busiest, if not *the* biggest port in Somalia. Plans include the construction of an entirely new docking station, specifically designed for smaller fishing boats, trawlers and travel boats. The planned location for the fishing boats at Bosaso port will be the specifically designated NEC FISH area within the larger port. The plans for the additional mini-port for exclusive use of fishing and travel boats is a welcome initiative, as it enables Bosaso main port greater freedom, efficiency and functional capabilities, which will subsequently boost commerce. Once the construction is executed, commercial vessels will have more space to dock and operate, while also enabling smaller boats a less congested space.

Moreover, the Puntland government has recently constructed a holding ground for livestock awaiting exportation and plan to install a beacon to direct incoming and outgoing ships, enabling the port to operate 24 hours each day/night.

Mogadishu Port: Mogadishu Port acts as a lifeline and a major source of internal revenue for the Somali Federal Government. As a result, it has been of immense economic importance to Somalia throughout its history. The port is administered by Mogadishu Port and Container Terminal (MDCT) and recently signed a deal with Simatech Investment worth around USD $170 million. Simatech is a logistics and container company based in UAE and Singapore with a proven track record in port management. It aims to provide more container services in Mogadishu port and to fully modernise the port, whilst improving its efficiency. In the past year there has also been interest shown by many international multimillion companies to invest in Mogadishu port and turn it into an international, world-class port - as it was in the past.

Berbera Port and the "Berbera Corridor": The port of Berbera is the single most important infrastructural facility in Somaliland and accounts for the bulk of the Somaliland administration's national revenue.

Strategically located, the port of Berbera connects East Africa to the Middle East. The port has a well-established, historical and strategic link to the Port of Aden in Yemen, due to the proximity of the two ports (separated only by 164 miles). Undoubtedly, Berbera Port is the economic hub of the entire autonomous northern state of Somaliland, a commercial centre in the region and one of the largest export centres in East Africa.

Export of livestock to the Arab world forms a major source of income. Although the Middle East is the primary location for exports, the port in actuality, imports as well as exports across the entire globe. The annual total of exports from the port equate to just over a million tonnes a year and also consists of staple foods, building material, consumer goods, etc.

In the past two decades, Berbera port has acted as a major outlet for land locked Ethiopia and it is no surprise to see that there has been much talk of a "Corridor" existing from Berbera in the coast to the Ethiopian hinterland, in order to capture the Ethiopian market and significantly improve trade links. The Ethiopian and Somaliland authorities have both been desperate to initiate this corridor for contrasting reasons. On Ethiopia's part, it has been landlocked since the De Jure independence of Eritrea in 1993 and with a population of over 80 million expected to double in coming decades, it is looking to branch out to further East African ports - other than Djibouti port - and sees Berbera port as a viable and profitable alternative. The Somaliland administration though wants to deepen economic and trade links with Ethiopia and access their market of 80 million consumers, indeed some economists have forecast that the Berbera port could account for around 30% of Ethiopia's national imports - which would boost Somaliland's import earnings by potentially hundreds of millions of dollars. More importantly they want to turn Berbera port into a regional hub that can compete against the world-class Djibouti port.

According to recent reports from African Review, the Somaliland authorities have signed a deal with French company Bollore Africa Logistics to invest in Somaliland's Berbera port with it investing USD $677 million. [60] According to the report; "*Bollore is about to*

---

[60] http://www.africanreview.com/transport-a-logistics/logistics/bollore-africa-logistics-to-invest-in-somaliland-s-berbera-port

invest US$677mn in Berbera port to improve the port and create a new corridor to the Ethiopian hinterland."

It has to be remembered that this development is in the formation stages, but it could enable the "Berbera Corridor" to maximise investment in the region.

In a recent development, the Financial Times (This is Africa publication) reported that the Somaliland authorities are in the final stages of ironing out an investment deal with a major port MNC (most likely Bollore Africa Logistics) to transform and fully modernise Berbera port.[61] Crucially, the report touches on how the establishment of the sought after Berbera Corridor will become a reality due to increased investment funds which may potentially total close to $1 billion in the coming few years. According to the report, of particular note is how in the long-term the MNC that is investing in Berbera Port intends to transform Berbera into a "regional logistics hub" worth potentially $2.5 billion and will act as a competitor against regional ports such as, Mombasa and Djibouti.

2. Infrastructure Challenges within Somalia

Investment: Since the late 1980s, there has been very little investment in the development or maintenance of transport infrastructure, due to ongoing conflicts in Somalia. The most important means of transportation, was totally worn out, either because of the war or many years of negligence during the former government. Airports and seaports have also been damaged and require extensive rehabilitation. In addition, due to the instability that existed amongst Southern parts of Somalia in the past two decades, this has led to a particular imbalance regarding urban road networks with the North-Eastern and Western parts of Somalia.

Linked back to our economic debate on Public Goods vs Private Goods, its clear that in the case of Somalia there has been little concentrated effort to invest in the infrastructure of the country. Regional governments such as Puntland and Somaliland have

---

[61] http://www.thisisafricaonline.com/Business/Somaliland-set-to-usher-in-major-port-investment?ct=true

made some effort, but again this was in no small part due to substantial, external donor funding.

Regulatory and taxation systems: More broadly, for the sustainability of the transport infrastructure sector, a regulatory framework (for revenue collection, customs, taxation and safety) would also need to be concurrently developed. The federal government is currently not institutionally powerful enough to formulate infrastructure regulation for development, maintenance or tax collection systems. In terms of Somaliland, they currently utilise road taxation, which they then use to maintain inter-city roads in major urban centres such as, Hargeisa and Berbera. Puntland also adopts this form of road taxation which serves to generate domestic revenue for the government.

In terms of Ports, both the Somaliland and Puntland governments efficiently tax their ports, Berbera and Bosaso, respectively. In the case of Berbera, the import & export excise taxes imposed, provide a key method of revenue generation and have always served to be a key issue of contention in Somaliland. In Puntland's case, with the ever-growing vitality of Bosaso as a port, it has succeeded in attracting many more clients and merchants than arguably Berbera and Mogadishu. The reason being that the Puntland government utilise a lower rate of tax at Bosaso port, compared to their competitors. Although these rudimentary tax collection systems for roads and ports do exist in Somaliland and Puntland, these methods still remain underdeveloped and loosely enforced, at best.

Technology and R&D: In terms of heavy equipment used to aid transportation infrastructure, the last time that this kind of machinery was invested in was under the Siad Barre government. However, a lack of spare parts and adequate facilities for repair and maintenance were major problems and finally most of this crucial equipment were plundered by the various warlords of the 1990s.

In terms of infrastructure development, Research and Development is a key component of development in a country's infrastructure. In Somalia's case, a post-conflict state that has only just emerged from civil war, such R&D has been neglected. In addition, if the government or regional governments within Somalia embark on infrastructural development, it is often the case that they have to import heavy machinery from China at a hefty price, which is also a very cumbersome process. In addition, despite the abundance of Somali engineers, there still remains a skill deficit in technology intensive subjects such as, engineering and computing.

Security: Conflict and insecurity present significant challenges to investment in urban infrastructure or maintenance of current systems, thus many landlocked areas such as coastal regions have suffered from an increase in the levels of insecurity, criminality and the impact of piracy. Indeed, it is no surprise to find a high correlation between isolation and areas with increased piracy or crime rates within Somalia.

Ad hoc planning: In major urban cities such as Hargeisa, there exists an ad hoc nature of town planning, whereby pressing issues are not addressed, such as water infrastructure and future water shortages. Hargeisa was a city designed to cater to 100,000 people initially during the colonial era and it currently caters to over 1 million inhabitants, which has led to serious infrastructural challenges that have not been addressed.

Such an issue is indeed evident in various urban cities within the country, for example, Mogadishu has the issue of IDPs which has led to public buildings and infrastructures being turned into makeshift IDP camps.

2.1 Economic Opportunities in Infrastructure

Due to the lack of railway infrastructure and limited coastal shipping within Somalia, road transport is the principal mode of internal transport. Camels and donkeys continue to be the only means of transport for many people.

With a deteriorating road network, air transport plays a growing role, which might become more expensive than roads. In order to consider road building and restoring roads, many regions in Somalia need to seek stability and peace in order to attract investment in infrastructure from the Federal Government or international donors. For instance, the establishment of a main highway coastal road going through the coastal regions from: Mogadishu, Cadale, Ceeldheer, Xarardheere, Hobyo, Garacad, Eyl, Bandarbeyla to Caluula - would boost regional economic development and could create employment for the local people within these isolated regions. Moreover, it could also improve public sectors such as: education, health, water, communication, social facilities etc.

Improved access to roads in these regions could also counter long-term issues such as increasing opportunities for reducing piracy and creating greater employment opportunities for youths.

With a coastline of about 3,300 km, coastal shipping has much potential and the development opportunities are multiple. Somalia's coastline carries 10% of the worlds shipping cargo. Sea transport and the expansion of fishing jetties and smaller ports (as a component of a broader strategy to address piracy), would provide alternate economic opportunities to piracy. On the other hand, it might attract interested international actors interested in opening up the Somali market.

It is recognised that there are several landlocked countries in East and Central Africa region such as: Ethiopia, Sudan, Rwanda Uganda and Burundi. Only two ports (Dar a salaam and Mombasa) exist in the region which can get highly congested, due to both supplying the whole region, However, Somalia also has the longest coastline in continental Africa and thus has a genuine opportunity to attract foreign neighbours to invest and support regional roads and ports infrastructure projects.

While the region currently is very attractive for development of oil and gas, the region lacks the sufficient transportation corridor to emerging markets such as India and China. For example Ethiopia, which has a population of 80 million and recently discovered gas in Ogaden, has a lack of maritime access or good infrastructure to export its goods. However, the Somalia coast could act as an opportunity for Ethiopia and other landlocked East African regions, which mostly have no access to maritime exports. In addition, there is also a number of high profile and potentially profitable investments in Somalia's transport infrastructure. Recently, Mogadisho port rehabilitation and the construction of Bosaso Air terminal provide visible examples of transport infrastructure being rebuilt.

In short, the potential economic dividends for firms investing in Somalia's infrastructure is indeed substantial. However, despite this, there has been a general focus specifically on the oil and gas sector, which is counterproductive, considering that infrastructural development is needed in order to benefit from the refinement and export of natural resources.

There is no doubt that Somalia as a state is situated in a strategically significant location, whereby it meets the Indian Ocean and the Red Sea. For example, Berbera Port is situated at the mouth of the Red Sea and is based in one of the busiest shipping lanes in the world. Therefore, for major foreign infrastructure specialist firms, there exists significant opportunities in Somalia - a country that lacks genuine infrastructure development. Indeed, there is currently scope for these MNCs to benefit economically by engaging in Public Private Partnerships (PPPs) with the government in order to provide these services.

3. Key Players & Public Private Partnerships (PPP)

Key Players: When researching Somalia's infrastructural development in recent years, it is clear that there are key players and forces which dominate the sector. Before touching on these key players, it is important for the reader to understand that Somalia is a post-conflict state which is currently at the reconstruction and recovery phase. This distinction is crucial in regards to infrastructure, because in most African states with stable, entrenched governments, there has existed the creation of powerful, state-owned infrastructure companies or boards which have dominated the sector. In Somalia this was the case prior to 1991, under the Socialist Siad Barre government, which constituted and utilised these powerful state-owned companies. However, with the collapse of the central government in 1991, and the increased privatisation of the Somali economy, such major, domestic key players in the infrastructure sector failed to emerge. The reason for this is linked to basic economics and the term "Public Good". In economic analysis, infrastructure is seen as a Public Good and as a result the sole responsibility of it falls on the government and the public sector, as it includes services (such as roads) which although beneficial are not profitable and require huge sums of investment. As a result of Somalia's lack of a strong, central government in the past two decades - regional governments aside - there has been very little development of infrastructure. In contrast, the private sector has only served to develop infrastructural facilities, which were key to their services, for example, telecommunication firms in Somalia created and expanded various telecommunication towers solely to increase their consumer base.

Therefore, in the context of Somalia's infrastructure, the key players have been donors and particularly the Turkish Investment Authority, which has had a strong presence in Mogadishu since 2011. Turkey adopted a strategic shift towards Somalia in early 2011 and its economic activities have been primarily confined to Mogadishu, where its infrastructural development projects are prevalent wherever one goes. The Turkish government was able to do this through its Turkish Investment Authority (TIA) which has channelled funds into building hospitals, schools, bridges, roads and Mogadishu's international airport. Current road development projects being undertaken by the TIA include the initial construction of a 23-kilometre paved road linking Mogadishu to Aden Adde International Airport which is now in its final stages.[62]

Another major donor has been the European Union Fund which has served to train and substantially fund the Somaliland and Puntland authorities to lead on their infrastructural projects. For example, the EU recently funded the Somaliland RDA in its aim to refurbish the Berbera – Hargeisa highway, which was in urgent need of refurbishing and modernisation.

Public Private Partnerships (PPPs): In short, PPPs are characterised by deals between public sector authority and the private sector, whereby the private sector is tasked with providing a public service or project and thus absorbing the costly financial, technical and operational risks inherent in the project. Even in developed states such as the UK, PPPs are relatively new and were only introduced there under the Thatcher administration in the 1980s. Yet, despite this, PPPs provide developing states such as Somalia with immense opportunities to overcome funding bottlenecks and to improve the state of infrastructure. This is because PPPs serve to address the main "financing gap" involved in expensive infrastructure projects and instead the efficiency and acumen of the private sector is utilised.

Within Sub-Sahran Africa, the use of PPPs to provide infrastructural development has grown by up to $11 billion in 2006 (World Bank, 2006). Therefore, it can be argued that PPPs as a

---

[62] http://sabahionline.com/en_GB/articles/hoa/articles/features/2013/10/03/feature-02?change_locale=true

form of financing infrastructure projects is relevant to Somalia as its infrastructure needs are extensive and the central government currently lacks institutional capacity to address these issues.

The main advantage of PPPs within Somalia would be to encourage and empower the ever-growing private sector to take on infrastructure projects, this is especially crucial in Somalia where the private sector accounts for as much as; 80-95% of economic activity.

In the case of the Somali Federal Government; if it adopts a systematic PPPs approach, then this in turn can lead to the adoption of innovative technology and efficiency as the private sector advantages and finances are vastly utilised. However, there currently appears to be little focus on PPPs within Somalia and the only exception can be found in the Puntland Development Plan which has a substantial focus on the adoption of PPPs to address infrastructure needs. [63] Furthermore, the Somaliland National Development Plan (NDP) has also focused on the utilisation of PPPs in order to alleviate infrastructural bottlenecks throughout the region.

The Somali Federal Government could use PPPs to build new road networks or renovate existing, worn-out road networks or to improve water infrastructure. Indeed, the central government can do this through financial incentives for private sector firms within Somalia such as, tax breaks. However, despite the success of private sector firms within Somalia, it is clear to see that such a monumental task of reconstructing infrastructure will require PPPs to be established with international private firms with a track record of completing infrastructural projects. This will enable the institutionally weak central government to improve the dire infrastructure of the nation, whilst allocating funding to other developmental needs of the state and stimulating the private sector at the same time.

Diaspora-led investments: During the past two decades; when Somalia was plunged into civil war, there emerged the phenomenon of diaspora-funded infrastructure projects. For example, in Taleex and other small towns there were small

---

[63] http://jplg.org/documents/documents%5CJPLG%20Documents%5CPPP%20Guide%20for%20Puntland-Jan2011-Short_Version.pdf

airstrips created to address those communities primary needs. In addition, other areas such as Las Qorey have witnessed diaspora-led investments such as the major fish factory. In addition; many roads within urban areas of Somalia have benefited from fundraising from diaspora communities abroad. A clear example can be found in construction of the Salahley Road, which connects Hargeysa to the largest district to the South near the Ethiopian border. In addition, diaspora-funded infrastructure and roads have long been utilised by communities within the Somaliland region and it is no secret that any infrastructure developments have succeeded due to diaspora investment, instead of government intervention.

Perhaps the single greatest example of diaspora-led infrastructural development at the moment can be found in the ongoing Burao-Erigavo Road which aims to create a road measuring around 300km passing inaccessible terrain. Through their public efforts, the Somaliland administration has managed to secure around $7.5million in donations and pledges from various Somali communities in Europe, North America and the Middle East and is currently in the process of raising funds for the remainder of the $30million needed for such a landmark road. Indeed, the Somaliland authorities have succeeded in embedding diaspora investment to their infrastructure development projects through the promotion of "Diaspora Bonds" and other such policies.[64]

The Somali Federal Government could use this model of diaspora investment and diaspora collaboration to encourage the development of infrastructure within Somalia in order to provide them with alternative ways to overcome funding bottlenecks for infrastructure development.

4. Summary

Infrastructural investment is critical for reconstruction and development in Somalia and key to enabling Somalia to develop rapidly. Particularly, it is crucial for employment and economic growth in a country where unemployment is commonplace.

---

[64] http://somalilanddiaspora.org/index.php?option=com_content&view=article&id=173:somaliland-new-investment-scheme-offers-exciting-development-opportunities

Transport infrastructure acts as the basis for the generation of income creation and solidifying trade networks. Hence, investment in transport infrastructure is key and an immediate priority. For foreign investors it is crucial that they seek to benefit from Public Private Partnerships which will enable them to work with the government in order to develop roads and various facilities. Indeed, in the long-term, such investment firms will benefit as Somalia currently has much potential in terms of its infrastructural development.

Due to its strategic location, Somalia can easily attract interested international investors and other African states that can utilise the country's ports, particularly landlocked regions such as: Ethiopia, South Sudan, Ruanda, Uganda or Burundi.

Indeed, it is no surprise that since Eritrea's independence in 1993, Ethiopia has been enticed by the prospect of the creation of the "Berbera Corridor" and the modernisation of Berbera port, which, according to reports, is imminent. Likewise, with the improving security situation in Mogadishu, it too has regained its status of a major port player in the East Africa region and has served to provide nearby ports such as, Kenya's Mombasa port, with stiff competition. The Somali Federal Government should focus on encouraging diaspora investment in infrastructure through Diaspora bonds or the creation of a Somali wide Diaspora agency, which can pool the financial resources of the substantial Somali Diaspora to assist in the development of infrastructure throughout Somalia.

Two and a half decades of conflict, concentrated mainly in southern Somalia, destroyed much of the country's governance structure, economic infrastructure, and institutions. Following the collapse of the Siad Barre government in January 1991, Somalia experienced deep cycles of internal conflict that fragmented the country, undermined legitimate institutions, and created widespread vulnerability.

In 2012, a new federal government emerged in Mogadishu within the framework established by the Provisional Constitution. Following the political transition in 2012 the international community agreed to the Somali Compact with the Federal Government of Somalia (FGS), based on the principles of the New Deal. The Compact, which was agreed to at the Brussels Conference in September 2013, provides an organising framework

(2014-16) for the delivery of assistance to Somalia in line with national priorities and increasingly delivered by Somali institutions.

Economic Development

Somalia's gross domestic product (GDP) is projected to reach $6.2 billion in 2016, GDP per capita at $450 and a poverty headcount rate of 51.6 percent. Consumption remains the key driver of GDP with investment accounting for 8% of GDP in 2015. Trade is important to Somalia's economy; the value of exports and imports taken together equals 76 percent of GDP.

The economy is highly dependent on imports, with the share of exports to GDP being 14%. Imports account for more than two-thirds of GDP, creating a large trade deficit, mainly financed by remittances and international aid.

Remittances, estimated at $1.3 billion, not only provide a buffer to the economy but also are a lifeline to large segments of the population cushioning household economies and creating a buffer against shocks.

Poverty is abundant with a half of the population living below the poverty line (51.6%). Remittances help reducing poverty. One in three people receiving remittances are poor (35.4%). Inequality is high, driven by the difference in poverty incidence in urban settings (close to 60%in Mogadishu and more than 40% in other urban settings) and rural settings (52.3%) with IDP settlements (71.0%). In 2015, 32% of the donor commitments were realized as a result of many factors, including lower oil prices and other bureaucratic hurdles. Domestic revenue is still insufficient to allow the government to deliver services to citizens.

Public expenditures have increased significantly since 2012, from $35.1 million to $135.4 million in 2015, driven by year-on-year increases in revenue. The government has shown improvement in domestic revenue collection.

Domestic revenue has grown by 36% in from $84.3 million in 2014 to $114.3 million in 2015, mainly driven by an increase in trade taxes. However, total revenue to GDP accounts for 2.8% of GDP.

The administrative and security sectors account for more than 85% of total spending, while economic and social services sectors account for about 10% of total expenditure. Poor collection capacity, narrow tax base, absence of the necessary legal and regulatory frameworks, and lack of territorial control hinder full revenue mobilisation.

Much of the population remains outside of the formal trade and banking sectors, and private investment remains extremely limited. Somali Diaspora remittances continue to be an important source of foreign exchange and economic support for the majority of Somalis.

REFERENCES

Chapter Two
The Somali Economy in Perspective

Orozco, M. Yansura, J. (2013). Keeping the Lifeline Open. [Online] Available: http://www.oxfam.org/en/policy/keeping-somalia-lifeline-open. [Accessed 19th Sep 2013].

FAO. (2013). Remittances and Livelihoods Support in Puntland and Somaliland. Available: http://www.fsnau.org/downloads/Remittances-and-Livelihoods-Sup- port-in-Puntland-and-Somaliland.pdf [Accessed 19th Sep 2013].

Gundel, J. (2003). "The Migration-Development Nexus: Somalia Case Study". In Van Hear, N. and Nyberg Sørensen, N. (eds) The Migration-Development Nexus. Geneva: IOM. [Accessed 21st Sep 2013].

Hansen, P. (2004) Migrant Remittances as a Development Tool: The Case of Somaliland. Migration Policy Research Working Paper Series No 3. Copenhagen: University of Copenhagen, Department of Policy Research and Communications.

Maimbo, S.M. (2006) Remittances and Economic Development in Somalia. Social development papers, conflict prevention and reconstruction paper No.38.

Kulaksiz and Purdekova (2006); Somali remittance sector: a macroeconomic perspective. Social development papers, conflict prevention and reconstruction paper No.38.

Somali Democratic Republic, Directorate of Planning, Ministry of National Planning. The Five-Year National Development Plan.

Menkhaus, K. (2001). Remittance companies and money transfers in Somalia,

United Nations Development Programme/World Bank Somalia, Socio-Economic Statistics, Somalia, Report No 1 Somalia Watching Brief 2003, draft.

http://www.nationsencyclopedia.com/Africa/Somalia-BANKING-AND-SECURITIES.html. Somalia - Banking and Securities.

CIA. (2013) Somalia. [Online] https://www.cia.gov/library/publications/the-world-factbook/geos/so.html#Econ. 2008. CIA World Fact Book.

http://somalbanca.org/. The Central Bank of Somalia. Monetary Policy.

www.eiu.com. Somalia Country Profile 2008. Economic Intelligence Unit.

http://somalbanca.org/financial-institutions/brief-history-of-the-somali-financial-institutions.html. Brief History of the Somali Financial Institutions. Central Bank of Somalia.

http://somalbanca.org/financial-institutions/brief-history-of-the-somali-financial-institutions.html. Brief History of the Somali Financial Institutions. Central Bank of Somalia.

http://somalbanca.org/financial-institutions/brief-history-of-the-somali-financial-institutions.html. Brief History of the Somali Financial Institutions. Central Bank of Somalia.

www.eiu.com. Somalia Country Profile 2008. Economic Intelligence Unit.

http://www.nationsencyclopedia.com/Africa/Somalia-BANKING-AND-SECURITIES.html. Somalia - Banking and Securities.

http://somalbanca.org/economy-and-finance.html

http://www.publicfinanceinternational.org/news/2013/06/good-financial-governance-crucial-to-somali-prosperity/

http://www.africanbondmarkets.org/countries/east-africa/somalia/overview/184/

http://fic.wharton.upenn.edu/fic/africa/Somalia%20Final.pdf

http://reliefweb.int/report/somalia/internally-displaced-persons-combined-report-somalia

http://article.sapub.org/10.5923.j.m2economics.20120101.01.html

Chapter Three
Telecommunications and Economic Policies

Bannon, I., Hahn, S. and Schwartz, J. (2004) 'The Private Sector's Role in the Provision of Infrastructure in Post-conflict Countries: Patterns and Policy Options' Conflict Prevention and Reconstruction No. 16 (Washington DC, US: World Bank).

Centre for Research and Dialogue (CRD) and WSP International (2004) Somalia: Path to Recovery (Mogadishu, Somalia: CRD).

Claire Pénicaud (2013), "State of the Industry: Results from the 2012 Global Mobile Money Adoption Survey," GSMA, London, UK.

Gruber, H. (2005). 'The economics of mobile communications', Cambridge, Cambridge University Press.

ITU (2005) World Telecommunication/ICT Development Report 2006: Measuring ICT for social and economic development. International Telecommunications Union, Geneva.

Little, P.D. (2005) 'Unofficial Trade When States are Weak: The Case of Cross-border Commerce in the Horn of Africa' Research Paper No. 2005/13 (Kentucky, US: University of Kentucky).

Nenova, T. and Harford, T. (2004) 'Anarchy and Invention: How Does Somalia's Private Sector Cope Without Government?' Public Policy for the Private Sector, No.280 (Washington DC, US: World Bank).

United Nations Development Programme (UNDP) (2001) Human Development Report 2001: Making New Technologies Work for Human Development (New York, US: UNDP).

Wellenius Bjorn (1993) "Telecommunications: World Bank experience and strategy" World Bank discussion papers. Washington, D.C.

World Bank/UNDP (2002) Somali Socio-Economic Survey 2011 (Washington DC, US: World Bank).

Yusuf, A. (2006). Somali Enterprises: Making Peace their Business. *International Alert*. P474 – 508. London, UK.

Anon, A. (2010). Hormuud Telecom. [Online] Available: http://www.hortel.net/viewpage.php?page_id=1. [Accessed 6th Sep 2013]

Farah, D. (2013). PennSID: Telecom Thrived Sans Governance. [Online] Available: http://www.pennsid.org/2013/02/telecom-thrived-sans-governance/. [Accessed 6th Sep 2013]

Shabelle Media Network. (2012). Somalia Gets 3G Mobile. [Online] Available: http://shabelle.net/somalia-gets-3g-mobile-service/ [Accessed 6th Sep 2013]

Anon, A. (2006). Golis Telecom Profile. [Online] Available: http://web.archive.org/web/20071022212418/http://golistelecom.com/about_g.htm[Accessed 10 Sep 2013]

Anon, A. (2005). Somalia calling: An Unlikely Success Story. [Online] Available: http://www.economist.com/node/5328015. [Accessed 10th Sep 2013]

Anon, A. (2006). Golis Telecom Profile. [Online] Available: http://web.archive.org/web/20071022212418/http://golistelecom.com/about_g.htm[Accessed 10 Sep 2013]

Anon, A. (2005). Somalia calling: An Unlikely Success Story. [Online] Available: http://www.economist.com/node/5328015. [Accessed 10th Sep 2013]

Yusuf, A. (2006). Somali Enterprises: Making Peace their Business. *International Alert*. P474 – 508. London, UK.

Chapter Four
The Energy Sector

Wawryk, A. S., 2003. International environmental standards in the oil industry: improving the operations of transnational oil companies in emerging economies. OGEL journal

Nwete B.O.N., 2006. Legal and policy framework for promoting petroleum expertise in Africa. Oil, Gas & Energy Law Intelligence(OGEL). Issue 4
www.somalieconomicforum.org – MAY 2012

Barnes, S. U., 1976. Geology and oil prospects in Somalia, East Africa: The American Association of Petroleum Geologists Bulletin. pp: 389-413. 11.

Fineman, M., 1993. The oil factor in Somalia: Four American petroleum giants had agreements with the African nation before its civil war began. They could reap big reward if peace is restored. Los Angles Times 12. Townsend, M. &

Abdinasir T., February 2012. Britain leads dash to explore for oil in war-torn Somalia. Government offers humanitarian aid and security assistance in the hope of a stake in country's future energy Industry. The Observer
http://www.guardian.co.uk/world/2012/feb/25/britain-oil-dash-somalia/print
nIRIN, March 2012. Benefits and risks of Puntland oil. Nairobi

Internet Pages

http://www.afdb.org/en/, www.boemre.gov, http://www.unep.org
http://www.undp.org, http://www.gasandoil.com/ogel/
http://www.ipieca.org/, http://www.bp.com, http://www.eia.gov
http://www.transparency.org/, http://www.norad.no,
http://www.irinnews.org/

Sources

African Development bank and the African Union, 2009. Oil and gas in Africa Commission (The National Commission on the BP Deepwater Horizon Oil Spill and Offshore Drilling), 2011. Part I: The path to tragedy. Chapter1 and Chapter 2. National Commission on the BP Deepwater Horizon Oil Spill and Offshore Drilling.
East Africa community secretariat, 2008. Strategy for the development of regional refineries
OIL WATCH AFRICA, May 2010. Oil Production in Africa: Livelihoods and Environment at Stake: Should Oil Rather Remain in the Ground?.
UNDP, 2009. Effective hydrocarbon management: lessons from the south
OPITO international, 2010. Growing globally: international report 2010 Available from opito.com
Wawryk, A. S., 2003. International environmental standards in the oil industry: improving the operations of transnational oil companies in emerging economies. OGEL journal
Nwete B.O.N., 2006. Legal and policy framework for promoting petroleum expertise in Africa. Oil, Gas & Energy Law Intelligence(OGEL). Issue 4
www.somalieconomicforum.org – MAY 2012
Barnes, S. U., 1976. Geology and oil prospects in Somalia, East Africa: The American Association of Petroleum Geologists Bulletin. pp: 389-413. 11.
Fineman, M., 1993. The oil factor in Somalia: Four American petroleum giants had agreements with the African nation before its civil war began. They could reap big reward if peace is restored. Los Angles Times 12. Townsend, M. & Abdinasir T., February 2012. Britain leads dash to explore for oil in war-torn Somalia. Government offers humanitarian aid and security assistance in the hope of a stake in country's future energy Industry. The Observer

http://www.guardian.co.uk/world/2012/feb/25/britain-oil-dash-somalia/print

nIRIN, March 2012. Benefits and risks of Puntland oil. Nairobi

Chapter Five
Infrastructure

East Africa community secretariat, 2008. Strategy for the development of regional refineries

African Development bank and the African Union, 2009. Oil and gas in Africa

Istanbul conference on Somalia, May 2010: Discussion paper for Round Table "Transport infrastructure"

Somalia: a country stduty3. Fisheries

The Economist Intelligence Unit (4th Quarter,1996).

Murphy M. N. & Saba J., 2011. Countering Piracy: The Potential of Onshore Development.

Puntland Five-Year Development Plan - 2007-2012 - Ministry of Planning and International Cooperation

Somaliland National Development Plan 2012 – 2017 - Ministry of Planning & Development

The Second İstanbul Conference on Somalia – Ministry of Foreign Affairs Turkey - June 2012

1St Somalia Investment Conference: Infrastructure, Security, Oil and Gas – June 2013

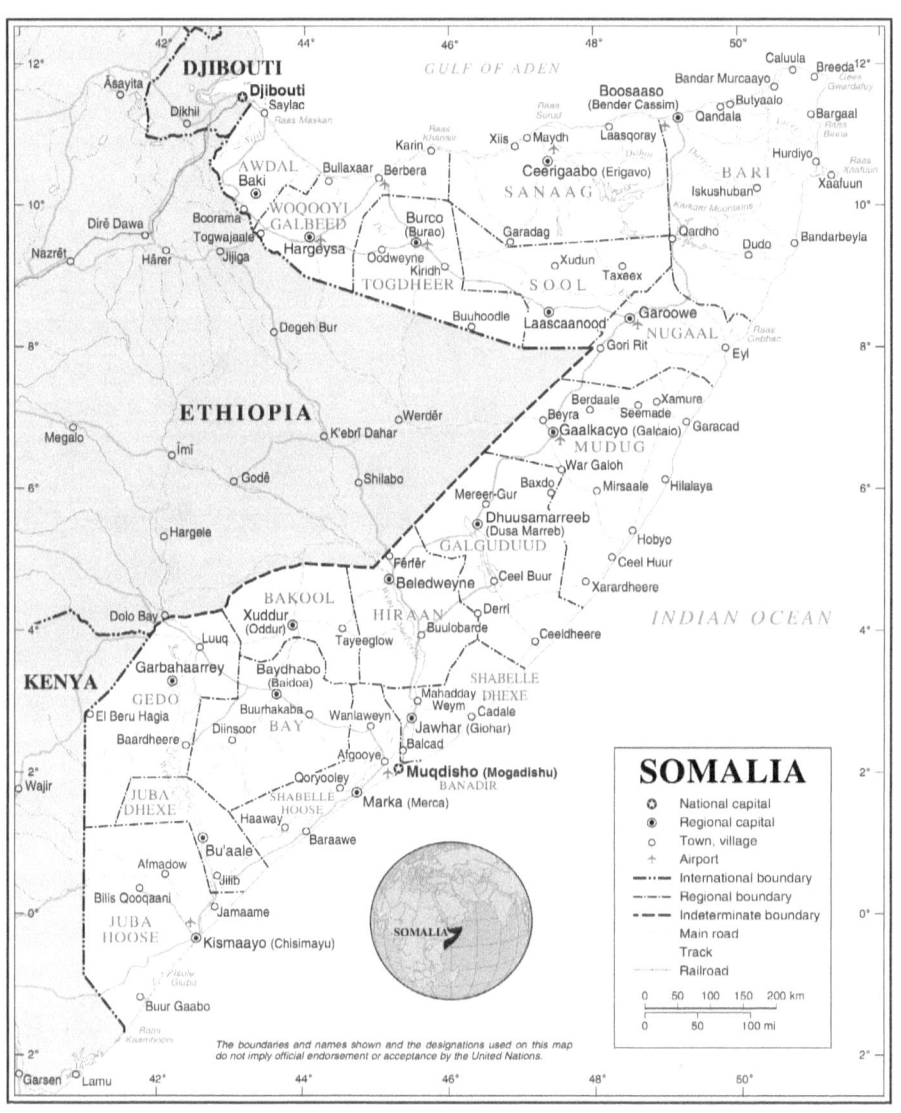

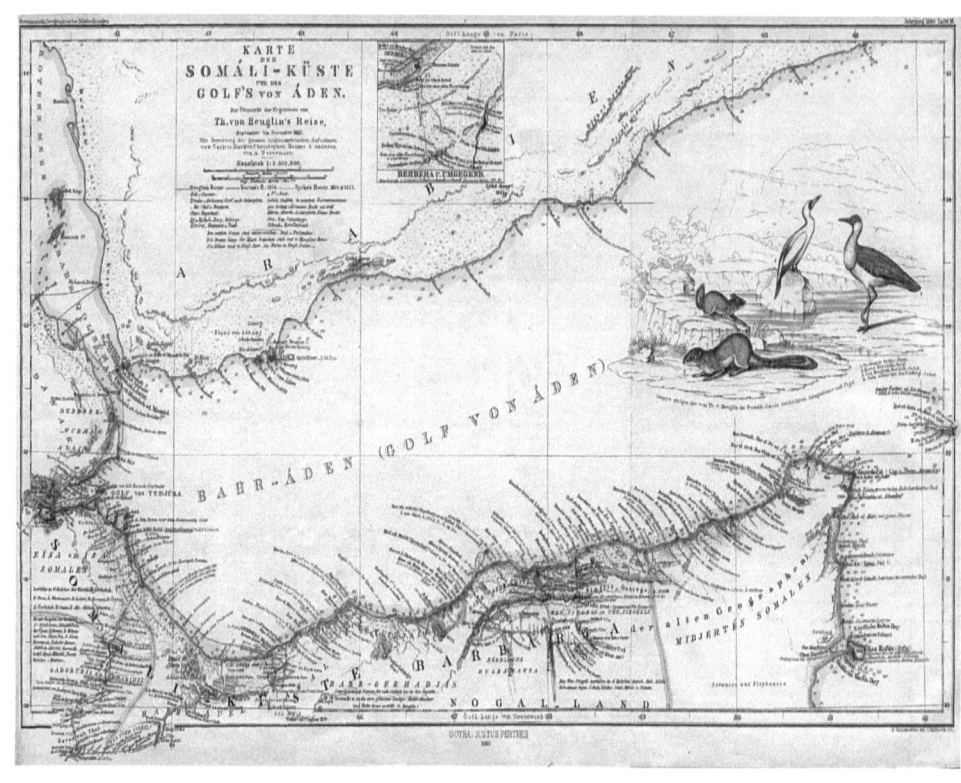

Somali Coast and Aden Gulf (1860)

About the Author

The Author, Hassan Musa Dudde, is known as Hassan Dudde. He is an economist and entrepreneur. Moreover, he is currently the Chairman & Managing Director of the Somali Economic Forum. The Forum was founded in 2011 to promote Foreign Direct Investment into Somalia, as well as pursuing research and publishing economic-related data on Somalia that is critical for meaningful investments. Hassan's background in economics and commitment to Somalia's economic recovery has placed him as an authority on Somalia, in Europe.

Hassan has advised a number of large international corporations and the UK government on trade and investment. Hassan worked with the Ministry of Planning and International Corporations on the Somali National Development Plan in 2016. He contributes frequently with regards to numerous debates on Somalia in various media platforms such as: Al-Jazeera, BBC, Radio France International (RFI), Bloomberg and Press TV. Hassan also contributes articles on Somalia's business and economy, which have been featured by the *Financial Times*, among other notable publications.

He graduated from the University of London, Queen Mary with MSc in Financial Economics and B.Sc. in Economics and Banking from University of Greenwich. He has worked in the investment banking industry in London since 2007 for Citigroup, Mizuho International, HSBC Global Asset Management, and UBS.

Dedication

This book is dedicated to my mother, Asli Khalif Nuur, and my father, Musa Dudde Samatar, who encouraged me in my education.

www.ingramcontent.com/pod-product-compliance
Lightning Source LLC
Chambersburg PA
CBHW030007190526
45157CB00014B/913